Flawless Execution

Flawless Execution

Use the Techniques and Systems of America's Fighter Pilots to Perform at Your Peak and Win the Battles of the Business World

James D. Murphy

1❿ ReganBooks
Celebrating Ten Bestselling Years
An Imprint of HarperCollins*Publishers*

HarperCollins books may be purchased for educational, business, or sales promotional use. For information please write: Special Markets Department, HarperCollins Publishers Inc., 10 East 53rd Street, New York, NY 10022.

FIRST EDITION

Designer: Nancy Singer Olaguera

Printed on acid-free paper

Library of Congress Cataloging-in-Publication Data has been applied for.

ISBN 0–06–076049–4

06 07 08 09 RRD 10 9 8 7 6 5 4 3

► IN MEMORIAM

IT IS WITH GREAT DESPAIR AND REGRET THAT WE HAVE LOST A
CORNERSTONE MEMBER OF OUR TEAM. STEVE "ROTHMAN" KENNY
WAS NOT ONLY A WARRIOR TO US ALL; HE WAS A FAMILY MEMBER,
FACILITATOR, AND, MOST IMPORTANTLY, A GOOD FRIEND. STEVE DID
NOT SURVIVE AN EJECTION FROM HIS A-4 SKYHAWK. THIS BOOK IS
DEDICATED TO STEVE. WE WILL ALWAYS HAVE ROTHMAN IN OUR
HEARTS AND ON OUR MINDS.

▶ ACKNOWLEDGMENTS

The fact that a fighter pilot can write one book should be cause enough for celebration; the fact that this is my second book shows the importance of teamwork! As with most things in life, this book was a team effort, and I have been blessed with being associated with many great and talented teams. I would like to take this opportunity to thank the many people who have been part of these teams and contributed to this work, and at Afterburner.

Big kudos must go to Doug Keeney, whose selfless hours, patience, and time spent with me coaching, editing, and guiding me through the process of becoming an author were invaluable. I especially thank my friend and partner Colonel John Warden and his staff for giving me the go-ahead to incorporate many parts of the Prometheus Process into this book and our teaching at Afterburner. Colonel Warden's work has truly been an inspiration to us all. To Mr. Walt Hauck, whom I consider one of the greatest business leaders I have met in my nine years of corporate training; your leadership at Pfizer and the incredible work you have done with the Infomatics team is nothing short of phenomenal. Thanks for validating our process, and thank you for all of your support.

To my close friend and business confidant Ron Bogdanovich, thank you for your time and effort in editing and keeping this book "real."

And most of all I thank the men and women on our team at Afterburner, whose collective intellectual property is the foundation of this book and our way of life at Afterburner. You guys are Sierra Hotel! Special thanks must go out to Michael "Pisser" Kenny for all of his great work on debriefing and execution. I also recognize the great things our Intellectual Property Board has brought to this book, so I thank these team members: Rick "Dewey" White, Charles "Skammer" Skoda, Dan "Razin" Cain, Matt "Whiz" Buckley, Cat "Radar" Peck, and Steve "Richter" McShea for all of your great work on the Flawless Execution Model.

To my partners—my wingmen, the best in the world, Anthony "AB" Bourke and George "Gundawg" Dragush—without your critical eye, unwavering mutual support, and insistence to strive daily to "Flawlessly Execute" in your lives and at Afterburner, this book would not be possible.

▶ CONTENTS

► FOREWORD

I am an American fighter pilot. I fly the United States Air Forces F-15 fighter, a supersonic jet with twin afterburning engines that ranks among the premier aircraft in the world. I can scramble to the jet, jump in, and, with just a few movements of my hands, crank up the engines, scan the 350 switches and dials in my cockpit, push up throttles to full afterburner, and in a matter of seconds be in a vertical climb and passing through 15,000 feet. Once I'm airborne, I am in command of a jet capable of dogfighting on either side of the sound barrier. I can climb high enough to see the curvature of the earth, or fly 500 feet off the ground in the black of night. Either way, when we're on a mission, when this plane and I are in our groove, it's comfortable; it's under control. I am one with this jet; I am defined by this intensely intimidating, highly effective, extremely lethal machine that can be sent virtually anywhere in the world.

The key word in that previous paragraph is "when"—*when* we work together. A supersonic jet is a temperamental beast. It is built for speed and agility. Those attributes give me a decided advantage in the air but I do pay a price for them. Fast and agile though the F-15 is, it operates inside an envelope that has razor-thin margins for error. This jet demands that I give it my undivided attention. It's constantly testing me. Sometimes I have just seconds to make choices that can save me or kill me. Fixate on one instrument and I lose the data from another—perhaps I fly it into the ground. If I don't listen carefully to the sounds this jet feeds me, I won't hear tones in my helmet or important radio calls from my wingman, and it's game over. Throw in checking my wingman's "six," terrain clearance, working my radar, weapons selection, navigation, making sure I know where the enemy is, and managing my avionics, and you can see how fighter pilots live and breathe the word "execution." I have to be sharp, alert; my situational awareness has to be crackling like fireworks. I have to sense and see things that ordinary people would not. In a nutshell, I have to execute—flawlessly—or this environment, this jet, this business of flying supersonic aircraft, will kill me.

That's the world of a fighter pilot. It's life at Mach One—fast, and in many ways thrilling, but absolutely unforgiving. Small mistakes can be lethal; our margins for error are tiny—there's just no room for a pilot who doesn't stay ahead of the jet. There's no room for sloppy execution.

That was then. Now is now. Now I'm a businessman. I specialize in the art of improving corporate and individual execution, which, simplified, is nothing more than the ability of one person to perform his task without repetitive mistakes. I specialize in this art because it's how I lived my life as an F-15 fighter pilot. If I failed to execute my mission properly, there was an incredibly good chance I was going to be a smoking hole in the ground. Not a nice day. The pursuit of flawless execution was the dividing line between life and death, between a successful mission and a scrub, between losing a wingman and bringing your squadron home together.

But was it so important in business? I thought it should be, but there were far too many examples around me that together seemed to say that flawless execution really didn't matter. Salespeople could have their sales pitches shot full of holes and suffer little more than the temporary misery of a long flight home. In the field, a technician or an installer or a repair man could spend two hours on a job site that required only one—and the company was no worse for the wear. And how many times had I seen a front desk clerk at a hotel or a sales clerk in a store bumble the most basic questions? I couldn't count. *In business, if you failed to execute your mission properly, there was always another day.* Sure, a promotion might be delayed, but the reality is, in the F-15, you die; in the boardroom, the corporate vice president has another day.

I started Afterburner, Inc. in 1996. I developed a training syllabus that demonstrated to corporate America how the unique tools used to train fighter pilots could be used in business to raise an individual's level of execution—as well as a corporation's. The better each individual executed, the more certain the corporate mission would be successful. As more and more people learned the tools and applied them, *doing their jobs as if their lives depended on it*, the more successful the company would be. Every mission, I said, was utterly and vitally important. Each salesperson, every front desk clerk, every installer, and every person in the marketing or manufacturing department was important.

In sum, our company set out to train a world of *corporate* fighter pilots—men and women who set the bar high, prepared for their mission, executed it as if their very lives depended on it, debriefed their experiences to accelerate their learning curve, and then went out and did it better the next time. I envisioned a world of *Leaning-Forward* dedicated, action-oriented men and women trained the way the United States military trains the most successful fighter pilots in the world—men and women with a passion for flawless execution.

Clearly, that message resonated with CEOs. By 2004, that idea I'd had eight years earlier had been turned into a bustling, multinational corporation ranking 212th on the *Inc.* 500. We were now fifty-one men and women strong, all of us training the average person how to do his or her job better. More than 100 of the *Fortune* 500 corporations have employed us to train more than 1,500,000 businessmen and women in the skills used by fighter pilots—skills that help them execute their tasks better than they ever thought possible.

The truth is, in business, tomorrow is not just another day. Second-rate standards, second-rate performance, and second-rate desire lead to the graveyard of corporate America. Capital markets dry up. Customers do walk away from poor customer service or marginal products. Compromise infects the organization. Revenues fall, companies suffer astronomical capital losses; there are decimated pensions plans and empty retirement accounts—and companies go belly up.

In my first book, *Business Is Combat*, I talked about the elements necessary to create a flawlessly executing *corporation*. I drew parallels to the highly successful organizational and executional tactics of the military aviation community. I spelled out how a company could create a fighter pilot "culture," a Petri dish that would nurture the growth of individuals and align them toward the company goals. I talked about how corporations needed to orient their assets—and indeed themselves—toward the execution of critical missions.

This book is different. This book focuses on the *individual*, and that distinction is very important. Great companies are built around extraordinary individual execution; the better the individual executes, the better the company performs. Take sales. If an individual improves its closing rates, the company benefits with higher revenues (and the salesperson takes home a fatter commission check to the family). In production, if an individual contributes to the overall manufacturing efficiency, the company becomes more profitable through reduced costs. Even simpler—in the hotel industry, if the individual at the front desk can correctly check in a guest the first time, the transaction will improve the customer experience, which will enhance the company's image, which in turn improves the likelihood that the company will enjoy repeat business from that customer.

It's all very circular, but it begins with how well an individual executes.

But individuals rarely act alone. Individuals are invariably part of a team; men and women invariably work in groups. Groups require leadership; individuals require missions and tasks. Then, and only then, this team of individuals executes as a group—a group measured on its collective execution, a group benefiting from the individual execution of each of its members.

Thus, the goal of the individual is to flawlessly execute. This in turn achieves the aims of the group—a flawless mission. When you do this over and over again, exceptional performance becomes a self-replicating strand of DNA that accelerates the evolution of the company into a higher species.

The results are predictable. You win and the group wins. And that is what this book is about. You will gain a trainable, learnable, repeatable process—*bred in military aviation*—that improves execution. It's about achieving Flawless Execution.

Flawless Execution

The Language of Flawless Execution

FLAWLESS (FLA-less): Without flaw; perfect. Syn: Faultless

EXECUTION (ek-so-KYU-shon): A carrying out; a doing; a performing.
Syn: Accomplishment

The ability to perform a task in the prescribed manner—Flawless Execution—is one of the most daunting yet vitally important missions facing corporate America today. With fewer workers underpinning the manufacturing base; with consumers demanding more for their money in terms of products or services; with intense pressures from the financial sector to meet financial targets, Flawless Execution has become the drumbeat of modern American business. How do we execute better? Is there a learnable, teachable, repeatable process to improve execution?

In fact, there is. It was developed in one of the most unforgiving laboratories in the world—the military jet fighter. In the aftermath of accidents, mistakes, and miscalculations that, since the 1940s, have cost uncountable aircrews their lives, Flawless Execution has become the theme in our book of lessons learned.

Born of necessity; due to the international conflicts that put our men (and now women) into harm's way, the United States military long ago came to grips with the need to train people how to execute flawlessly. Nowhere was it accomplished with more fervor, with more thought or study, or with a more fanatical dedication to institutionalizing the results than in the training of America's fighter pilots.

To understand Flawless Execution, you must first understand the language. Throughout this book, I use language that is different from what you'll find in corporate America, and here's why: Too many corporate words carry around baggage that I want you to shed. I don't want you to assume that you know what I mean when I use certain words, so instead, I use the words that we pilots use when executing our mission. Why? Language from the pilot's world will be largely new to you, so I can fill each word with the exact meaning I want you to have. Let me give you an example.

The Flawless Execution Model is based on a pyramid. The pyramid describes how a "mission" is executed. The heart of the pyramid is the execution engine. Here we introduce you to a cycle called the Plan-Brief-Execute-Debrief-Win cycle. Each of these four "phases" leads back to "Win," where the process starts all over again. Visualize these words as five points on an ever-connecting, ever-looping cycle. To achieve Flawless Execution, every task will have a specific Plan-Brief-Execute-Debrief-Win cycle.

Now, I could have used words like "analyze," or "implementation," as one might in the corporate world, and if I had, I would be understood before another word came out of my mouth. But that's not what I want. The Plan-Brief-Execute-Debrief-Win cycle is quite different—and infinitely more powerful—than the regime of Plan-Implement-Analyze. With it you have a mecha-

nism that thoroughly prepares you for your mission, gives you a list of scripted responses for contingencies, and contains *the most powerful weapon in business*—the debrief. At the end of every mission, the entire team sits down and debriefs. Mistakes are identified, root causes are unearthed, and a better way to do things works its way right back up into the planning cycle that begins the very next day—or the very next hour. Imagine the advantage. On a four-day sales trip, lessons learned from day one are built into the planning for day two. Learning experiences are accelerated; individual performance is supercharged.

Let me give you another example: At the top of this pyramid is the starting point. It is called Future Picture. Now, you may think you understand what I mean by Future Picture, but throw out whatever you're thinking because we're talking about the *Flawless Execution* definition of Future Picture. Future Picture is a high-definition picture that shows in great detail the future as you want it to be. We paint this picture in a resolution high enough to let any level of management, or any team member, zoom into it at any detail and find within it clarity, composition, and texture. This is accomplished by crafting a twelve-point descriptor, each word of which has purpose and meaning that when dissected withstands microscopic scrutiny. The Future Picture is a statement of what you intend to have happen.

The perfection of that picture is in detail—detail fine enough to give your team information sufficient to visualize how their personal contributions will help attain that picture. The Future Picture governs both group and individual execution. Because it's richly textured, it neatly interlaces with latitude, the proper amount and degree of which individuals must be given so that as they execute, they can adjust their execution *within the boundaries of the Future Picture* to ensure Flawless Execution. What are these boundaries? They will vary, that's for sure, but every task, every mission, every job we perform has to contribute to the attainment of the overall Future Picture even when (not if!) we encounter a problem. The trick is preparing for problems by having a portfolio of contingencies planned out in advance that, when used, nevertheless move us forward toward the Future Picture. Let's throw out the more rigid, organizational words of objectives-strategies-plan for the simpler, leaner, more dynamic, and ultimately more realistic guiding principle called the Future Picture.

This raises an interesting point. How does latitude work in a model called Flawless Execution? Good question. The answer is this: The Flawless Execution Model is not a model in pursuit of the elusive "five 9s." Humans are not machines. Rigid executional tactics work in machines, but they do not work in humans. Humans need flexibility. Humans innovate, adapt, improvise— sometimes to a preplanned "contingency" script—but machines don't. Five 9s may be attainable in a "closed" environment like a computer, but it isn't in humans. Flawless Execution is not the pursuit of perfection; rather, it is the pursuit of a method of operation that, when done correctly, can be replicated by the organization. Latitude, therefore, recognizes our human nature. Latitude, when exercised against a clear understanding of the intent of the organization (or the mission), lets people overcome obstacles that with rigid rules would be insurmountable. It allows the individual to inject initiative and training into a situation even as the rules change. Think of it as a football game. A receiver runs a broken pass route, but instead of giving up, he executes a preplanned alternate route and the pass is completed. It wasn't the play called in the huddle. It wasn't flawless. But the process delivered a flawlessly executed play nonetheless, and the team achieved its goal of moving the ball closer to the end zone.

Then there is something we call *Standards*. Again, toss out your old definition. How often has a golden opportunity unexpectedly arisen for which you were ill prepared? I was going to the bank to make a deposit and as I walked down the sidewalk, I happened to walk into a client I'd been trying to talk to all week. Was I ready? You bet. I had a practiced, polished elevator pitch ready to go—and I had the delivery, the inflection, the choice of words I'd used based on the situation I was in, down to a science. But here's the neat part—every one of my partners was as prepared as I was and each of them would have kicked into the same pitch. Would you be ready? Do you have a well-practiced pitch you could deliver in the brief time of a ride in an elevator? Could you go into action and deftly turn that chance encounter into a valuable opportunity? By practicing standards, a chance encounter can be as productive as a full-blown sales call planned months in advance. I'll tell you in a later chapter about a California F-16 fighter pilot who ended up flying Combat Air Patrol over New York City on September 11, 2001, with the Vermont Air National Guard—a pilot no one in Vermont had ever met before, all because of Standards.

Which leads me to training and people. As you explore the Flawless Execution Model, you'll be introduced to a new way of looking at training and a new way to accelerate the competency of your people. The Air Force believes in finding the right person with the right skills for the right job. That done, they like to send recruits up the learning curve as fast as they can. Why? Because we live in a dangerous world and the sooner new pilots overcome the experience curve the better. The Air Force does that by using a series of feedback loops called Lessons Learned, catalyzed by an invaluable process they call the Debrief. You and your people will overcome learning curves too—if you throw away your old notions and understand exactly what I mean by a Lessons Learned and Debriefs.

This, then, is the language of Flawless Execution. New words; new meaning to old words. Put aside your assumptions and let these new meanings become a part of your higher-achieving lifestyle.

The Flawless Execution Model

Reproduced with permission by Afterburner, Inc.

Flawless Execution is like the perfect round of golf: always attempted, never attainable, although pieces of it may be perfect along the way. But for me, and for the countless fighter pilots out there, it defines our way of life. We are *always* in pursuit of flawless execution. Pursuit is our way of life.

Let's unpack that. A mission in an F-15 is a complex undertaking with countless variables. More often than not, several jets will be assigned to a flight, and each will have a designated role. Variables. We will be supported by tankers and intelligence aircraft and other aircraft with other supporting roles. More variables. The target is, of course, hostile, which presents dozens of even more complex variables, some good, but most of them bad. Add it up and the probability that a mission will unfold flawlessly is probably one in a billion. However well trained we are, however well planned the mission, a mission is always imperfect—the number of variables is astronomically high. Maybe one of our air refueling tankers was at the wrong rendezvous point or one of the planes in my four-ship had to abort, or maybe I had a maintenance problem with my jet. Perhaps the weather changed en route and the target was obscured or the enemy had more defenses than we expected. Or maybe it was something as simple as a radio transponder failing on one of the jets. The point is that something always goes wrong. When you break down a mission and examine it in minutia, there are a lot of mistakes in a so-called flawless mission.

That's fine. That's the way it is. But remember, we're always in pursuit of Flawless Execution. Things go wrong, but we still take out our target and we get everyone home safely because we expect things to go wrong, and expecting things to go wrong is part of the definition of Flawless Execution. In the air, at every step, we pilots correct, adapt, and come up with solutions because we're prepared for the unexpected. We know a flawless mission will be riddled with adjustments, changes, and variables.

In truth, that's not much different from everyday life. Look at sports. I like the way one great basketball professional said it: "Murph, you give up a lot of points on the way to winning a game." Of course you do! There is no perfect golf round, no perfect basketball game, no hitter in the major leagues who bats 1.000. Flawless Execution doesn't mean you do things so well that you smoke the opposition; it doesn't mean your opponent is going to roll over; it certainly doesn't mean things won't go wrong. *Flawless Execution is all about expecting things to go wrong—and handling it.* In aviation, I had a model, a method, a repeatable process that kept me alive. Instead of becoming a smoking hole in the ground, I had scripted responses to some really ugly scenarios and subtle but dangerous problems. That's Flawless Execution. I lose a lot of points on the way to winning the game, but I win more than I lose.

BUSINESS IS COMBAT, COMBAT IS BUSINESS

Every Afterburner seminar begins with a comparison. I was a fighter pilot for the United States Air Force; you're in business. What could we possibly have in common?

First let me tell you a little about flying a fighter. Today's military fighter aircraft is a sophisticated piece of machinery that is capable of speeds in excess of 1,200 miles per hour. This machine wraps around the pilot, the sole human component. It has wings, a tail, a fuselage, and engines that generate enough thrust to lift twenty or thirty thousand pounds of dead weight straight up in the air without missing a beat.

But that's not the purpose of this machine. The purpose of this machine is to deliver weapons against a hostile target. Bombs, missiles, bullets. We're equipped to use any of these.

There's no graceful way to get into this jet, but these planes are tough. Pilots can walk on their wings (and I did) or grab the canopy rails with our full weight. When I at last slid down into my seat and settled in, I was in a snug cocoon of technology with not an inch of room to spare. This was my office—the cockpit. In front of me were 350 instruments and lights and displays and switches, and around me were the throttles and the control stick. Behind me were two big engines ready to kick out a twelve-foot blowtorch when I pushed the throttles into afterburner. On the ground, the F-15 is a thing of beauty. The jet is sleek and seems genetically tuned to work through the skies. The cockpit is a synapse, a ganglion, needing only a human to complete the node. How can you not admire the perfection of it all? The ergonomics. The sensible layout of the instrument panel. The interrelated functions of my hands, my feet, and all the instruments.

But then again, I wasn't paid to sit in the cockpit and admire the engineering any more than you are paid to sit at your desk and admire the computer and file cabinets that surround you. I was paid to fly this thing. I was paid to let my fingers move over those toggles and switches, to listen to calls through my helmet, to watch for enemy missiles and fighters, while my afterburners put a bone-crushing force on me that compressed my lungs and pushed blood from my head, sometimes blurring my vision so much that in a high-speed turn the edge of the instrument panel turned gray. I was paid to ignore the shuddering vibration of the airframe as I yanked and banked the jet during a dogfight; flew a high-speed, low-level pass through a mountain valley; or tucked into a close formation at night in bad weather with an air refueling tanker.

With all that going on, the loudest noise in my helmet was usually the sound of me struggling to breathe. It's risky. It isn't for the faint of heart. Seven out of ten trainees wash out of training before they even touch the skin of an F-15. One otherwise fit reporter had to be extracted from a jet after a demonstration flight with the Thunderbirds. He stayed in the hospital for two days.

So what's the message here? Am I a tough guy? Not at all. When I first flew the F-15 I was twenty-three years old. I was a college kid with okay grades. Fifteen months before I flew the F-15, I had never touched an airplane. I'm no math genius and I'm probably no better coordinated than you. I stay in shape but, on the average, I'm probably in no better shape than you. But I went through a process. I followed a process perfected over more than five decades that made me a fighter pilot.

The United States Air Force is a direct descendent of the Army air forces of World War II, and it became an independent branch of the armed forces under the Department of Defense in 1947. What ensued was a period of constant change. Jets quickly replaced piston engines. From a slow, subsonic air force we became a fast, supersonic air force. We received better radar and new weapons; we were flying higher than anyone thought possible and our airframes changed every four or five years.

But it wasn't going that well. Accidents were on a steady climb until in 1952, we had our worst year ever—1,214 airmen were killed in accidents. Planes were crashing, wings were coming off, pilots were losing control, and entire flight crews were being wiped out before lunch. It was a disaster.

In fact, training was our Achilles' heel. We weren't doing it right. We were slow to keep up with the slew of new aircraft arriving on our flight lines and we weren't giving pilots a way to think through their problems before they evolved into accidents. Thankfully, the Air Force reacted. They began to focus on the capabilities of the human mind and the capabilities of the human body to manipulate an aircraft in flight. How many G-forces could a pilot withstand before he blacked out? How many instruments could we scan? How long did that scan take? Did we understand the information our instruments were feeding us, or should we change the way instruments displayed data? All of these were called "human factors." Human factors became a major body of study. It touched how aircraft were designed, how cockpits were laid out, and how we were trained. It became a dynamic process. It evolved into a process called Crew Resource Management (CRM). How does a pilot or a flight crew assimilate and process the information in the cockpit and manage the data between pilot and copilot?

Whatever the name, human factors or CRM training, the product is training. Training procedures are updated and then updated again. Training is a science. Training has intensified. It is part of our everyday lives, and instead of just flying, we became a force of pilots that *train*. The results were dramatic. By 2002, the most recent year for such statistics, we were flying more missions than ever before, but even so, the accident rate was a mere fraction of that horrible year, 1952. In 2002, we lost just nine airmen. Enough said.

As a former fighter pilot, I can say without boasting that I know what it's like to execute flawlessly—but I'll go even farther. In today's military, 98 percent of our aviators know that feeling. And that's what we teach at Afterburner. We transfer our experiences and techniques from military aviation to business to show you how to achieve Flawless Execution. We know what it is like to experience disaster, and we know the great feeling of a job well done. We believe in Flawless Execution and we allow our lives to depend on it. We make Flawless Execution a process that governs us. When we get up before an audience at an Afterburner event and talk about our world, we do so because, as fighter pilots, we are the very proof that Flawless Execution is achievable. That's our point: Our way works.

Like the exhilaration a marathon runner feels when he crosses the finish line, we feel the exhilaration of executing flawlessly. In Desert Storm. In Afghanistan. In every training mission we fly. We have a Leaning-Forward, got-to-win, don't-accept-mistakes attitude, and it's all focused on one outcome: a flawless mission. If we can do it in the 1,000 mile-per-hour, fast changing, and extremely hostile world of air-to-air combat, you can do it anywhere. Simple message. It's what over 1,500,000 men and women have learned from us. Flawless Execution built the most successful military aviation organization in the world; Flawless Execution can make you and your company as successful as you want to be.

Our specialized training aside, we both have jobs to do. I was part of an organization whose business it is to protect this nation. The USAF has a headquarters in Washington and two major commands under it. It has branch offices called air wings and within those air wings are air force bases. On those bases are squadrons. Within each squadron is a commanding officer. Squadrons have budgets and goals and are accountable back up the chain to the wing commanders, who in turn are accountable to the commander-in-chief and to the American people. The USAF's work is closely tracked by the media, by Congress, and by the intelligence agencies of other countries. Their mistakes are scrutinized under the glare of the press; their triumphs largely go unnoticed.

That's the business side of combat. Like you, I was measured by outcomes when I was a fighter pilot. I had my missions; you have your missions. I had a target and a plan of action to hit that target. You have a plan of action to hit your target. If I failed, likely I'd die. If you fail, you're looking at a short career. We're not so different. We both need to execute.

Execute. In this day and age, *execute* is a word that takes on a special meaning. During the dot-com bubble, time was everything. Shoot-aim-fire was the order of the day. Execution was replaced with immediacy. We need to get in the game. We need to launch this company immediately. No one wanted to miss out. No one wanted to be left behind, and venture capitalists threw money at plans for companies and products they didn't really understand.

And no one remembered that someone had to execute. Someone had to deliver the goods. Little wonder that the dot-com bubble burst and the remains of tattered, ill-conceived business plans were scattered everywhere. As fast as you can punch out with an ejection seat, the venture capitalists tucked in their tails and fled.

Then came the corporate scandals. Again, one of the root causes was the absence of any real execution. Instead, someone was cooking the books or layering in false front corporations for bogus transactions to make it *look* like they were delivering the goods. Enron collapsed on inflated sales. WorldCom collapsed on inflated sales. Qwest restated billions in revenues. Adelphia. ImClone. And the list goes on and on. Instead of hard-working, dedicated, determined people doing their jobs, poor execution was covered up by illegal practices that made the companies appear to be executing flawlessly.

Now times are tough and we're back to basics. The economy is short-winded but showing promise. Companies have fewer people than they did a year ago. There is an urgent, pressing need to run businesses smartly, to get the job done, to deliver the goods, to execute with good business practices. Speaking before countless corporations across the nation, I see this daily. Frustrated CEOs come up to me and ask: "Murph, how do I get my people to do what they're supposed to do? How do I improve execution?"

That's why we stand before you in our flight suits. That's why we talk to you about our jets and our missions. It is designed to underscore the differences—and the similarities. Fighter pilots have jobs to do; you have jobs to do. Supersonic jet fighters engaged in combat *must* execute flawlessly or we stand a good chance of dying. So we've found a process for doing just that and we've seen it work in combat and now in business. So, trust me, we're not asking you to do anything we haven't already done. We're proof that against seemingly astronomical odds, people can execute their missions flawlessly. We do, or we die. Every day.

It's true: Being an American fighter pilot is hard—but being our enemy is a lot harder. The Flawless Execution Model gives us an unfair advantage.

An Introduction to Flawless Execution

I was standing in the hall outside one of our seminars when a senior executive of a major manufacturing company flagged me down. His products were selling well in the general retail trade accounts, but they were terribly underperforming in the large chain accounts. He thought he knew why: The chain buyers had their own way of doing business, and his regional managers just didn't seem to be sophisticated enough to handle them—but he wasn't entirely sure.

His solution was to hire a national account manager. Unfortunately, the new national account manager met with stiff resistance internally. Most troubling of all, the resistance was coming from his very best people, the men and women he trusted the most. "Why send in someone from the home office who doesn't even know my client when I see my client every day and know what he needs and when he needs it?" said one manager. Another said, "National chains are the one chance I have to earn big commissions. Now you're going to take that away from me?"

To say the least, it was upsetting to my client and it had created a dangerous rift in the company. The sales force was dangerously distracted and my friend was perplexed. On the one hand, a national account manager could give his products the singular focus he thought they needed to better perform in the chain accounts, but it was equally true that the territory rep knew the customer better; after all, it was their territory.

"What should I do, Murph?" he asked.

I didn't have a clue. And even if I had, if I gave him an answer, what would he have gained? I'm not in the business of welfare; I don't give out food stamps. In flight school we aren't given answers; we're given ways to *find* answers. We're given processes, patterns, and ways to think things through so we can come up with our answers on our own. So I had a little fun. I sat him down and we talked. "What's your overall Future Picture for the company?" I asked.

He told me. "Good." I said.

"What are the key strategies to attain your Future Picture?" I asked. Again he answered. Also good.

"Do each of your departments have a plan and a process for executing?"

Silence.

I tried another tactic: "Help me understand why you need a national accounts manager."

Because, he said, his sales weren't nearly as strong in the national accounts as they were in small stores.

"Okay," I said, "and why is that?"

Because the salespeople felt uncomfortable with the chain buyers, he said.

"How do you know that?" I asked.

It was obvious from their poor market share, he said.

I pressed on. "What does the national account buyer want that keeps tripping up the sales force?"

He thought a minute. "Deeper discounts," he said.

"Why can't you give them deeper discounts?" I asked.

"We sell in one-, four-, and eight-packs. We can't give deeper discounts unless they order more quantities—and they don't want to order more."

"What do they want?" I asked.

"They want a unit with more products in it," he answered

"And how did you come to that conclusion?" I asked.

"I heard about it in the annual sales meeting from several of the managers," he answered.

"So, is this a staffing problem or a product problem?" I asked.

And that's when his light turned on. Here we were, dealing with a major, unplanned obstacle that was blocking his salespeople from doing their job, dealing with it in the middle of their sales planning conference, in the hall, coming to terms with an issue that had been dividing the company for almost three months. He didn't need a national account manager; he needed a line extension. He needed a twenty-four pack or a forty-eight pack or something big for the big box store. But more importantly, he needed a *process* to feed data back to him faster, directly, raw and untouched. He needed a *process* that let him see the complete picture and solve his problems on the fly, which is exactly what exists in the fighter pilot world.

In 1990, Saddam Hussein invaded Kuwait and President George H.W. Bush, along with most of a very angry free world, was outraged. As we all know, Bush took action. Inside the Pentagon, he gave his military commanders a simple order: "Get Iraq out of Kuwait." Clear enough, said his commanders, so off they went to the planning staff and told them that the president wanted Kuwait liberated. *Click.* A *process* went into action, a process that would stay in action until the very last soldier returned to his or her home after the battles were all over. Iraq would be forced out of Kuwait, allied casualties would be held to a minimum, and the job would be done in the quickest time possible with as little collateral damage as practicable. Inside that big, tumbling, chaotic mess called war, a process would stay in place, one that would answer the hundreds if not *hundreds of thousands* of tactical questions like the one my CEO friend was asking me in the hall.

We had a system in place to expect the unexpected, to anticipate obstacles but provide a pathway to answers when the plan went afoul. Let's say that a small cog in this enormous cycle was to take out the enemy surface-to-air missile sites—the SAM sites. Not easy, but we knew how to do that. A weapons system called the F-16 Wild Weasel would do the job nicely. All we'd have to do is get that F-16 across a long stretch of hostile air space over to a hostile SAM site so he could fire a missile down the radar beam and take it out. While he'd be doing that, the pilot would have to dodge a fusillade of return fire with his back exposed. With all the turning and burning, he'd certainly run out of fuel before returning to friendly airspace.

Our commander knew all this, but when he stood up before us, all he said was: "Ladies and gentlemen, this is what I want to do. I want to wipe out every Iraqi SAM site in this kill box in three days. You understand what I want. You know the intent of your mission. I don't care what it takes. Just make it happen." Now, obviously we got more information than that, but once he'd communicated his intent, that's pretty much all we needed to know; we went to work. We began the process called Plan-Brief-Execute-Debrief-Win. We used it when we trained. We used it when we flew in combat. It was second nature to us. First, everyone involved in the mission got involved in the planning. The Intel people collected intelligence on the SAM sites. The F-16 Wild Weasels got terrain briefs, updated their targeting plans, and loaded HARM (High-speed Anti-Radiation Missiles) missiles on their jets. Because we didn't want them exposed, we tasked a four-ship of F-15s to sweep the area for Migs before the mission and then escort the package during the mission. We also had some KC-10 tankers to refuel us.

The elements of the mission took shape.

Once each team had its plan, we coordinated them and then briefed each team in minute detail. Timing was always important, so we started with a time check. Then we went through each and every step of the mission—the threats, the weather, the contingencies, the problems we may have, and the exact way we'd handle those problems, all the way down to who refueled first on the tanker and where the others would wait until they got on the boom to refuel (in this case, two in formation off the left wing, one off the right wing).

From the briefing, we executed that mission. What is execution? Execution is nothing more than flying the brief. It is the unfolding of a scripted play. If all went well, we'd take off, hit the air refueling tankers, fly to the kill box, eliminate the SAMs, and return to base within a minute of the briefed time line. If that wasn't how the mission went, we had contingency plans. For instance, if we were attacked by enemy fighters, we had a plan. If one of the Wild Weasels had to abort, we had a plan. If two Wild Weasels aborted, we had a different plan. If we had too many problems, we had a plan for shedding tasks—shedding until we were down to the essentials to accomplish the primary mission. (We even had a plan if the sunlight created too much glare!)

Execution is the unfolding of a play scripted down to the last second.

When the mission was over, each one of these teams had a nameless, rankless debrief, which was an extraordinarily powerful part of the process because each of these units immediately broke down the mission and looked for ways to improve their execution. We looked for root causes attributable to even the slightest misstep and then came up with a list of lessons learned. Then, unlike that CEO I talked to in the hall, we had a mechanism for feeding those lessons learned directly into the next planning cycle *even if the next mission was headed out in a matter of hours*. (In fact, it can go even farther. If that lesson learned was so important, if it could save the lives of another flight crew, we would feed that lesson learned up or down the chain of command to all of the fighter squadrons in the wing, a process that accelerated everyone's experiences, everyone's learning curve as if they'd flown that mission with me that day risking their own lives. In the end, we all execute better.)

Remember: No mission is perfect. Let's say we didn't get all the SAMs. In the debrief, the pilots might be saying, "The intent was to take out the SAM sites, but three are still up and this is what I learned from the mission today: The intelligence guys forgot to tell us that mobile Triple A might be in the area. We Wild Weasel guys, therefore, had no reason to brief a contingency plan called a multi-axis attack. Had we done so, we would have reverted to our contingency and the mission would have been executed as briefed. Feeding that lesson learned back into our next brief should result in the full achievement of our objective— taking out the SAMs in the kill box."

That's how debrief moves information back into the planning process and keeps you accelerating learning experiences and constantly improving. In fact, if you took only the top lesson learned from each one of those squadrons and funneled it back into the system—all the way up to the leader—then the leader would have a chance to understand what went on and massage, change, or tailor the intent to make the next mission even more effective.

We did this every day for every mission. We were always tightening our plans, getting smarter, adapting, pulling off the next mission a little easier than the last. This is how we adapted and stayed one step ahead of the competitive rate of change in our environment. This is how we accelerate our learning process, keep our pilots alive and move one step closer to flawless execution, something my CEO desperately needed in his company.

Sadly, this is something businesses do poorly. Our experiences with the top corporations in the world bear this out. *Businesses rarely see execution as a process and almost never debrief.* What a mistake. Without that process, without that debrief, mistakes are glossed over and those valuable lessons learned do not go back up the ladder to the leaders. In a fighter pilot's world, this process is everything. That's how we keep pilots alive. That's how we win wars.

As I said, it was, and no doubt is, hard being an American military fighter pilot. It's dangerous. But it's a lot less dangerous than being our enemy. Our jets may be no better than the Mig-29s and Sukhoi SU-31s but we have a process no air force in the world equals. Future Picture. Strategy. Leaders Intent. The Plan-Brief-Execute-Debrief-Win cycle. All supported by our standards, our training, and our people.

So does this work in business? How does it work in you? Let's look at the model again.

Reproduced with permission by Afterburner, Inc.

In business, think of the Flawless Execution Model as a tool for energizing *systems*. After almost ten years of corporate training and coaching some of the world's top companies, I began to see a problem. Most companies had smart and competent leaders who were passionate about their work and focused on their company's success. They had employees working hard to do the job and fulfill the company's mission. But rarely did these organizations execute like we did in our squadrons. Why? These same companies said they had great strategy, and their people were the best in the industry—so why the lack of execution?

I quickly realized that "strategy" was the most misunderstood and misused word in corporate America. My first book, *Business Is Combat*, was about aligning your team or organization around a very clear mission, which is critical to winning in combat as well as in business. If you execute flawlessly against the wrong things and never get to your end goal, you can have the best tactics and the most passion, and still lose. In this day and age of doing more with less, finding out what those "right things" are that we need to execute against is even more critical.

This did not go unnoticed by the United States Air Force. During the weeks leading up to Operation Desert Storm, a brilliant Air Force fighter pilot, Colonel John Warden, was tapped by General Chuck Horner, then Chief of Staff, to plan the air war. Warden mapped out the Iraqi "system," narrowed down the number of prospective targets from several hundred thousand to just the critical targets, then tested the plan against the Future Picture—get Saddam Hussein out of Kuwait. General Horner liked what he saw, and the plans were approved. In action, the plans spawned a level of execution that few battlefields have ever witnessed, then and now.

I met Colonel Warden three years ago. In the years since retiring from the Air Force, John has spent his time distilling the techniques he used in the Air Force down to an understandable body of knowledge he calls the Prometheus Process. As fellow ex–fighter pilots applying our techniques to the business world, we saw a fit between our focus on execution and his interests in systems, centers of gravity, and Future Pictures. As one fighter pilot to another, we started to blend our messages, even our minds.

As Colonel Warden has discovered, every company is a *system*. Every industry is a system. Every division operates as a system. Even your body operates as a system. They all have interrelated parts. To achieve success, all the parts have to work in concert. It's like a car. A car is a system. If the wheels fall off, the car won't work—the *system* has broken down. Same with you. You may make it to a meeting with a buyer, but without your sales literature, you're system doesn't work and you're reduced to becoming the cliched glib salesperson with his hands flapping in the air.

A systemic approach is key to the Flawless Execution Model.

How does a system work within a corporation when you employ the Flawless Execution Model? Let's use a common corporate process—a competitively bid contract—as an example. Let's say a contract is up for providing catering services to a sports stadium. The request for proposals (RFP) goes out to a dozen highly qualified companies. The contract is for sixteen retail food outlets in a major sports stadium. The sports stadium wants to know your credentials relative to the bid, a detailed list of your menu items, the variety, the quality of service you'll guarantee, and of course, what their slice of the revenues will be.

Management wants it; you want it. The contract is worth upwards of $5 million. Winning the contract fits into the overall Future Picture for the company and certainly supports the leader's intent, so you assemble a team to prepare the bid. Who do you bring in? You need the facilities people to lay out food stations and the placement of the equipment, and to analyze the flow of food from the freezer to the customer. You need the signage people to come up with an abbreviated version of your normal store signage. You need the menu people to consider the actual food items that will be listed for sale. You do time management studies to make sure the products can be prepared quickly so you avoid the death spiral of unhappy customers waiting in long lines. The finance people have to look at margins and royalty rates. The supply chain people need to study the influx of business in a compressed time frame and determine how they will make sure the raw ingredients are there for each item. Human Resources has to map out a plan to train the counter people and the grill chiefs. Special considerations have to be made for the surges in traffic at the intermissions. And each one of these "departments" has to figure out what the competition is going to do and how they can beat their proposal.

Each of these departments, or "silos," meets and, together as one, attacks the specifications of the RFP. Is it war? You bet. You ask yourself all of those tough questions. How much royalty should we pay the stadium? How much will the competition pay? How many menu items do we need to have to make our bid competitive? How much capital will we have to invest? What does the overall picture look like when we're up and operating?

Then you get the good news. You won. Now you're in the execution phase. Now you have to perform. Are you ready? Guess what? The planning process made you ready. Because you had everyone involved in the planning process, you have universal buy-in to the execution. The purchasing department starts purchasing and the signage people start writing contracts and when an obstacle comes up, you find out about it during the day's debriefing. The lessons learned get fed back into the next day's planning cycle, continuously, right up to opening day, right through the entire season, right up until the last sale is made for the season. As in the military, you start writing standards and the process stays in place; it's scaleable. Every day the concessions operate a little better, the flow of raw materials is a little smoother, worker satisfaction goes up, customers like your people—the *system* works.

At the heart of the Flawless Execution Model is a circular, continuous process you're involved in every day. You take a general Future Picture, map out the system, identify centers of gravity, and break it down into a plan that each Flawless Execution team or business unit can execute to accomplish the overall future picture. The marketing department, the packaging department, the manufacturing department, and the R&D department take the Future Picture and create their own process in support of the intent. If one area falls out—let's say they're taken out by a bomb, or they get outsourced to another company—progress toward the final outcome is not decapitated. When there's a problem, it gets fed back to the planning stage immediately.

When everybody's involved in the process, you suddenly have a very powerful, replicable, scalable organization, one where people can replace people and new initiatives can come online smoothly. The alternative? We call it the bricklayer syndrome, where you lay a brick but never know exactly what the architectural design of the house is.

This is how it looks from the 30,000-foot level. Now let's break it down and apply it to your business.

CHAPTER 4 ▶▶▶✈▶▶▶▶▶▶▶▶▶▶▶▶▶▶▶

Future Picture

Individual execution is one thing . . .
organizational execution is everything!

Reproduced with permission by Afterburner, Inc.

Flawless execution begins with a Future Picture. What is a Future Picture? Said simplest, the Future Picture is a view of the future as we'd like something to be. That *something* can be a new company, the person you want to be in three years, or the reorganized mega-corporation that needs to adapt to change. It's a well-written, clear, high-resolution, and easily communicated picture of what you want the future to be.

When I start to explain what a Future Picture is and what we are going to expect it to accomplish, I ask our seminar attendees to indulge me in a little exercise. I ask them to plan a picnic. What could be easier than planning a picnic? I ask one person to come up with the menu, one to pick the drinks, one to select the transportation, and one to pick the location. After a couple of minutes I ask them to lay it all out for me. As you might expect, each person had a different idea on what the perfect picnic should be. Our menu planner thinks it's a table filled with platters of cold cuts and cheeses, and our drink planner likes beer. The transportation planner picked limousines, but the location planner picked a park.

And I thought a picnic was red checkerboard tablecloths, hamburgers on the grill, and horseshoes.

At this point I show them a slide of Pierre Auguste Renoir's painting *Luncheon of the Boating Party*.

In this magnificent piece of art we see one man's Future Picture of a picnic. We see men and women in festive attire on a barge cruising through the countryside, drinking red wine, eating fowl on thin-crust crackers spread with caviar. We see netting for the bugs, a linen tablecloth, glass stemware, and everyone wearing great hats. Had I shown the group this painting before we began our planning and said I wanted our picnic to reflect this painting, what kind of answers would I have gotten? Menu: rolls, thin-crust crackers, various dips and crab meat, caviar, and a roasted chicken. Drinks would include Perrier, pinot noir, white wine—and lots of it. Transportation would be by boat. Location—we'll embark from the banks of the river at the yacht club.

Renoir provided the team with a high-resolution Future Picture of a picnic. Anyone on the picnic planning team could look at it and answer any of the countless questions that need answers when organizing a picnic. The richness, the completeness of this Future Picture is what makes it work. It becomes a beacon. It pulls people in a common direction toward a common goal as articulated in a Future Picture having sufficient content and clarity to provide guidance down the ranks. Executing is not enough. You must execute in the spirit of a Future Picture or you will invariably execute against the wrong things.

Think about being at the ballpark and asking your friend to order a hot dog for you. Your friend may go down to the concession stand and execute the order to the best of his ability but what he doesn't know is *your* vision of a hot dog. Is your vision of an awesome hot dog one on a plate or a hot dog wrapped in paper? Does it have pickle relish on it? Do you like mustard, onions, or green peppers? Is your idea of the perfect hot dog a big half-pounder or is it a slim hot dog like the ones you had as a kid? Are you following me? What you have in mind is your Future Picture of a hot dog: pickles, ketchup, onions, on a plate, with two napkins—and it better be a big half-pounder. In order for your friend to get this right, did you paint a high enough resolution picture to make this a reality?

Entrepreneurs are by default the masters in the art of painting Future Pictures. Why is this? It's because entrepreneurs sell vision. They don't have a company. They don't have offices or sales. So they have to paint a high-resolution Future Picture of their vision and use that Future Picture to convince venture capitalists to part with their money and cajole partners to join them—maybe even get lenders to lend them money, vendors to give them credit, and employees to join them. Entrepreneurs sell the future. They "see" the profits, the building that has a sign across the top with their name on it. They "see" the glowing magazine articles that will be written about their corporate culture or about their tireless energy or about how great they are with customer service, product design, or clever marketing, or maybe even the impact they've made on the economy. If they can't paint a vivid, powerful, detailed, textured Future Picture, there will be no company.

FUTURE PICTURES: SOME EXAMPLES

In 1990, Saddam Hussein ordered his troops to invade and seize control of Kuwait. The egregious act of aggression horrified the world and a coalition of forces was organized under the command of President George H.W. Bush. On the eve of a military operation in the Middle East, President Bush gave his commanders a clear Future Picture: "Iraq will be out of Kuwait. Allied casualties will be low. Collateral damage will be minimized (so Iraq can recover quickly). Saddam's Army will not be a regional power for at least ten years. Oil will flow freely in the region." Pretty simple. Very direct. Easy to understand, and yet, it's a Future Picture with resolution and detail sufficient to give his commanders a starting point for the planning process that would lay down the specific strategies necessary to achieve his Future Picture.

Let's look at what President Bush did not say. President Bush could have said: "I see a future where the Middle East is stabilized." Noble. Admirable. Easy to understand. But how would one translate that into an action plan? How does a military operation proceed? It doesn't. The Future Picture is too general. There is no focus, nothing to act on, no leverage points.

At the other extreme, President Bush could have micromanaged the process. He could have said, "I want fleets of B-52 bombers dropping bombs, Navy ships launching F/A-18s on the hour, and all of our soldiers on the ground attacking Baghdad relentlessly pouring shells on government buildings until they agree to sign an armistice." To do that it would probably take all of our B-52 bombers and most of our soldiers, and it would, of course, handcuff our military experts. Moreover, by inserting a condition for the end of the war, the Future Picture turns the power over to the enemy.

No, instead of either of these Future Picture statements, the commander-in-chief empowered his best minds with a simple but clear Future Picture, and the results were nothing short of phenomenal. To this day I would contend we have never been involved in a more successful military campaign.

What about the business world? Let's look at Amerada Hess; they sell gasoline. Ten years ago, maybe fifteen, that's about all they sold: gasoline. But the industry evolved and they successfully made the migration to the convenience store-plus-gasoline model and were thus able to increase the average sale per customer. So far so good. But, over the years, the margins on gasoline were shrinking and the basic business of the tobacco, candy, and soft drinks store was under the gun. Moreover, every Tom, Dick, and Harry was getting into the gasoline business. Kroger. Wal-Mart. You name it. So, not only were margins slim but volume was shrinking, too. How do you survive? How do you grow revenues and maintain profits when the business is going elsewhere and the margins are razor thin? Future Picture.

The CEO of Amerada Hess saw a future where the very survival of his stores depended on his ability to make his stores a far more desirable place to go to than a Kroger or a Wal-Mart or, for that matter, any other gas station. To survive, better yet, to thrive, his thousands of outlets had to be viewed as more than a place to buy gas and incidentals like tobacco and candy. He saw something radically different. Wal-Mart was a destination store; why not Amerada Hess? In the CEO's Future Picture, Amerada Hess would be a *destination*. Drivers would leave their homes (or hop off the interstate) to go to an Amerada Hess gas station for all of those things that we need but likely don't want to suffer the hustle and bustle of a grocery store or a Wal-Mart to get. Make our stores a destination, he said to his managers; give the people in our adjoining neighborhoods the products they want. Give it to them in a self-service environment that's clean, with a shopping experience that's quick. And, oh by the way, don't charge more than the local grocery store but make me a good return on my money. After that, he left it to his vice presidents to iron out the details, which they did. First they studied their customers and found out what they wanted, talked to designers, and worked on the layout of the stores and the positioning of the gondolas and shelves. They worked on their retail appearance, redesigned logos, and put together the pieces that made gas stations into convenience stores.

Today, they are called Hess Express. Listen how the company described these remarkable stores: "The newly opened Hess Express convenience *centers* represent the state-of-the-art of this retail expression. They are consumer destinations in their own right. This is accomplished by offering a blend of traditional convenience store items, a proprietary gourmet coffee, and nationally branded fast food services in a physically attractive presentation that is both high-tech and friendly" (www.hess.com). Hess Express is a place you go to for high-quality fast food like TCBY, Godfather's Pizza, or Blimpie. They have a wide assortment of groceries and sundries. The merchandising is attractive. The stores are absolutely clean. The transactions are smooth. The training of their service staff is continuous. Quality is a high priority. And the target audience is the family. "Fast, fun and family oriented" is their mission statement. The results? Despite a bleak economy and a competitive universe where it now seems everyone is selling gas, Amerada Hess has recorded consecutive quarterly increases in revenues and profits that are the envy of the industry.

That's Future Picture. The Future Picture gave the corporate mission planners a clear picture of the future that the CEO saw in his mind. With that picture, each of the internal silos started to build their plans—marketing, advertising, business development, product development, store design, purchasing, training, and so on. Weaving those plans together had only one possible outcome: Hess Express is now a destination shopping experience.

Rule 1. Focus on the Future

A Future Picture statement opens the door to creativity and outside-the-box thinking at exactly the right moment in the process—before anyone has locked down plans and started the execution phases. It also *focuses* the commanders *on the future.* If it doesn't contribute to the Future Picture, it doesn't belong on the table. If it doesn't contribute to pushing Saddam Hussein out of Kuwait, it doesn't belong on the table. If it doesn't make me want to go to a Hess Express, then why are we talking about it? This is the purpose of a clear Future Picture. It is designed to draw out the best of an organization while at the same time serve as a beacon, an aiming point for everyone's actions.

Rising out of the ashes of the battered telecommunications industry is a true phoenix. It's a technology called 802.11 or "Wi-Fi" or wireless. Wi-Fi is a low-cost, fast-deployment, radio-based infrastructure that can deliver broadband Internet connections to businesses and residences. It can as easily connect entire rural towns as it can your laptop to the Internet at a Starbucks. Read the press and you'll see a story about it. Wi-Fi has certainly been a disruptive technology.

But that's today. Three years ago few people knew of Wi-Fi. It was relegated to a few tinkerers in their garages. Venture capitalists had no interest in it.

One entrepreneur had a different Future Picture. He saw a future where broadband would travel through the air wirelessly to connect people anywhere, yet cost just half of what the big companies were charging. His Future Picture of wireless broadband was not unlike Herb Kelleher's of Southwest Airlines. It's not about the planes. We all have the same planes. It's about being affordable, reliable, and fun.

Taking a well-textured Future Picture, the entrepreneur engineered a network using this forlorn technology called Wi-Fi, painted his picture before angel investors, and raised a few million dollars. Soon he had hundreds of customers flying onto the Internet across his low-cost wireless infrastructure and he was taking money and market share away from the local DSL and cable modem providers. And not just one entrepreneur was doing it. Dozens, then hundreds, of entrepreneurs saw the same thing. All across the nation they started to build their own wireless Internet data networks. The FCC loved it and opened up the rules to encourage even more investment and even more deployments. Venture capitalists started to listen to the story; monies flowed into business plans. Future Pictures were refined and evolved. Wireless Internet providers are now approaching 10 percent of the Internet connection market—and they were nothing more than a playful idea five years ago.

Rule 2. Key Descriptors: Painting with Colors

How do we develop a Future Picture? Colonel Warden studied this in detail, looking at the attributes that made the military process work so well, then observing the behavior of business organizations. Warden merged the military processes with the organizational needs he identified and came up with a list of key descriptors that make up the Future Picture. Renoir would call them the colors on his palette. In either case, there are exactly twelve key descriptors that must be included in your Future Picture.

1. **Financial Position.** Describe your company's financial position as you would like to be in a reasonable amount of time,

say three to five years. Will you measure internal rate of return (IRR), earnings, revenues, EBITDA (earnings before interest, taxes, depreciation, and amortization), or what?

2. **Market Position.** Describe your market position. Will you be a leader or a follower? Are you a fringe segment? Elaborate.

3. **Business Areas.** What business(es) do you intend to be in?

4. **Innovation.** Will you innovate or use off-the-shelf technology? Is R&D part of your future?

5. **Insider Perception.** What is the insider view of the company? How do the various stakeholders view the company? Is it a good place to work, a good investment? Elaborate.

6. **Outsider Perception.** What should the outsider perception be? A growing company, profitable, customer-oriented? Professional, competent?

7. **Workforce Characteristics.** What are the features of your workforce? What are their skills, special talents?

8. **Brand: Yes or No.** Are you going to have a branded product or a commodity product? Will you be an OEM (original equipment manufacturer) to another company?

9. **Corporate Culture.** What is your vision of your corporate culture? Are you entrepreneurial with a minimum of bureaucratic layers? Are you productivity driven like Dell Computer?

10. **Corporate Citizenship.** What is your vision of corporate citizenship? Will you make a contribution to the quality of life in your communities? Why?

11. **Ownership.** Will your company be public, private, or have an employee stock plan?

12. **Incentive Philosophy.** What will your incentive plans be based on? Straight pay, shared risk, rewards based on results?

In developing the Future Picture, we blend those twelve key descriptors into a detailed picture of the company. The results don't have to portray a dramatically different company or in any manner go over the top. Future Pictures are horses-for-courses—they're unique to you; they're unique to your company. But they need the twelve descriptors. Again, the Future Picture is a view of the future as we'd like something to be. That "something" can be a new company, the person you want to be in three years, or the reorganized mega-corporation that needs to adapt to change. It's a well-written, clear, high-resolution, and easily communicated big picture of what you want the future to be.

Future Picture is a beacon that pulls the team into the designed future.

Future Picture Sits on Top of the Flawless Execution Pyramid

Viewed within the Flawless Execution Model, the Future Picture is always at the top of the pyramid. It is the starting point for mission execution, and it is the end point. *Get Saddam Hussein out of Kuwait. Keep allied causalities low. Reduce Saddam's military's effectiveness. Get oil flowing again.* That tells us what we need to do and what signifies success. Now we communicate.

Communicating the Future Picture across the organization assures management that everyone knows what the company is intent on doing. Confident in the knowledge of what their company wants, people can draw up and execute their own plans. They know what type of hot dog you want. They understand your vision of the perfect picnic—you won't sit down to a platter of cold cuts on the ground with ants crawling over everything; you'll be in Renoir's boat excursion. The Future Picture sees to that. The Future Picture ensures that your Flawless Execution teams will not be executing against the wrong things, things of their own experiences or past performance, but toward the future you intend.

Future Picture is the starting point for Flawless Execution.

Rule 3. Measures of Merit

To achieve the Future Picture you must attach to each key descriptor a succinct measure of merit. What are measures of merit? Measures of merit are the measures of success we attach to each key descriptor. These are the things that have to happen in order to achieve the key descriptors, which in turn, realize our Future Picture. They tell us we're making progress—that the future is materializing.

Measures of merit are absolutes, not comparative, and are written to focus on strategic progress versus any sort of tactical success. They are clear, concise, and easily communicated.

In the section on key descriptors (Rule 2) we talked about branded versus nonbranded. If your key descriptor painted a Future Picture with a product that is branded, a concise, absolute measure of merit might be a high product rating by J.D. Power or high product awareness among the target audience.

If your financial descriptor called for profits that doubled in three years, a measure of merit might be a quarterly measure of EBITDA, or, better yet, net profits.

No matter what you choose, the measures have to be strategic, not tactical.

Here are some examples of Future Picture key descriptors and their measures of merit (MOM):

Financial Position
- **Key Descriptor:** Double Profit and Equity in three years.
- **MOM:** Non-EBITDA and company value doubles within three years.

Market Position
- **Key Descriptor:** Number one brand in segment.
- **MOM:** Market share hits 80 percent; competitors scramble to copy.

Business Areas

- **Key Descriptor:** Highly differentiated integrated products; no commodity products.
- **MOM:** Profitability selling our catalog products; not manufacturing or selling commodity products.

Innovation

- **Key Descriptors:** R&D creates and patents next-generation products.
- **MOM:** Portfolio of next-generation patents filed; multiple requests to license.

Insider Perception

- **Key Descriptor:** The place to invest our time, energy, and money.
- **MOM:** Insiders buying stock; multiple applicants for all positions; lights on all night.

Outsider Perception

- **Key Descriptor:** Profitable, growing, customer-oriented company.
- **MOM:** Earnings per share growing at 12 percent per annum; bookings, revenue, and profits up.

Workforce Characteristics

- **Key Descriptor:** Passionate, self-starters well educated in technology and business.
- **MOM:** Multiple volunteers to speak on company's behalf; multiple proposals for new business lines accepted.

Brand

- **Key Descriptor:** Well known by customers and end users.
- **MOM:** Customers and end users request our products by name.

Corporate Culture

- **Key Descriptor:** Entrepreneurial with minimum bureaucracy and focus on productivity.
- **MOM:** Everyone within four levels of CEO; CEO overwhelmed with smart proposals; productivity up from $300K per employee to $600K.

Corporate Citizenship

- **Key Descriptor:** Contributions to the communities we serve.
- **MOM:** Letters of appreciation for company volunteers in local papers and from local officials.

Ownership

- **Key Descriptor:** Everyone a stockholder.
- **MOM:** Treasurer's records compared to payroll.

Incentive Philosophy

- **Key Descriptor:** Reward results with money; recognize effort with thanks.
- **MOM:** Bonuses paid to top individual and team achievers; hard workers recognized daily in bulletins and meetings.

CHAPTER 5 ▶▶▶▶✈▶▶▶▶▶▶▶▶▶▶▶▶

Strategy

You can have the best execution in the world . . .
but if you execute against the wrong things you will lose.

Reproduced with permission by Afterburner, Inc.

Whether you're planning an air war or the launch of a new product, strategy is the connective tissue between the Future Picture and the individual plans that your execution teams will develop.

Unfortunately, strategy means a lot of things to a lot of people, and rarely do any two agree on the definition. Let's look at how we'll be using it.

ALIGNING EXECUTION TO STRATEGY

Most people don't understand strategy. I was a speaker at the annual meeting of the International Council of Air Shows (ICAS). Before me sat hundreds of incredibly talented pilots consisting of aerobatics teams, outstanding individual civilian performers, plus the very best of the various military flight demonstration teams, including no less than the Navy's Blue Angels and the Air Force Thunderbirds. These were people who were like me—people who live and breathe Flawless Execution. Every one flew an aircraft and executed a performance that, if done wrong, could kill them. So, here I am before my brothers and sisters ready to deliver my standard keynote, but today my job is to get them thinking about the air show business. How does their act contribute to the overall Future Picture of an industry that puts on more than 200 air shows a year? How does what they do help build a product with the brand appeal and uniformity and the shared revenues of the NFL or Major League Baseball or NASCAR?

I started with strategy. My hunch was that almost no one in the audience was thinking strategically about the business side of the air show world. "You guys can fly a perfect show and flawlessly execute your mission," I said as I began. They nodded. "You're flawlessly executing, but are you helping achieve the overall strategy of the ICAS show you're performing in? Are you aligned with their Future Picture? Probably not."

I put up a slide. It showed dozens of arrows pointed in different directions. I continued.

"Imagine," I said, "that each one of these arrows is one of you. Look at it. You're working hard and doing a great job. You're flying your solo act or your four-ship formation aerobatic team perfectly and no one can fault you on a thing. You people are a bunch of hot sticks executing your acts with absolute precision. My hat's off to you.

"But, what about the big picture? Imagine that each of these arrows had a rope tied to the overall ICAS organization. See what's happening? All of those arrows pull in different directions. Yes, you're executing flawlessly up there; you're flying your act absolutely perfectly. But is your act aligned with the Future Picture of the ICAS organization? Do you even know what their Future Picture is? NASCAR controls everything from the racetrack to the cars to the uniforms the drivers wear. Each race has a standard level of quality, predictability, rules. The drivers—sure, they have personality and would probably like to come out with cool names like Gravedigger or maybe have a PR team of attractive girls doing wet T-shirt contests behind the pits. But they don't. So, have you noticed what sport has absolutely exploded? NASCAR. Why? Because NASCAR delivers a consistent product. The fans are in the stands because they know the race will be a loud, rocking-and-rolling, consistent, family experience. No matter where they are or what race they attend, they know the venue will have vendors selling this and that and the drivers will line up for autographs at a certain hour and that nothing offensive is going to happen when they least expect it. Things will be clean. The uniforms worn by the drivers will be professional-looking. The cars will be freshly painted. Everything is controlled by NASCAR with one thought in mind—consistency."

I looked over a room full of great pilots, but I wasn't talking about flying. I was talking about aligning. I continued: "Have you assigned ICAS the rights to license merchandising and products; have you given them control over your brand name? Some of you wear flight suits and look sharp and some of you are wearing T-shirts and jeans. Some of you are selling high-quality merchandise next to your planes, and some of it, well, it's awful. Sure, you are all executing perfectly but you're doing so against your own Future Picture, your own parameters. Isn't that about right?"

I paused to look around. The faces I saw were slowly nodding acceptance. I continued. "Isn't that what's going on at the average air show? Everyone's flying a flawless performance but there's no cohesion, no alignment behind a common strategy. Do you see any cohesive, collective strategy? Of course not," I said. "Arrows are going in every direction, all flawlessly executing, but not aligned." Then I asked them to participate in a demonstration. "I want each of you to gently put a hand on the shoulder of the person next to you," I said, "and give them a slight push." One by one they tentatively raised a hand and did what I asked.

"Now, while you're pushing, look around." They looked around.

"See what's happening?" I said.

See, indeed: Everyone was leaning in a different direction.

"Now I want all of you to *lean in this direction*," I said, leaning my body to the left, "and now put a hand on someone's shoulder and push again."

Guess what? They were all pushing in the same direction. Did I tell them which hand to use? No. Did I tell them what direction to push? No. But the entire room was leaning in one direction.

Satisfied that I was getting their attention, I put up another slide. The arrows were more or less pointing in the same direction. "You see," I said, "with just a high-level statement, what we call a Future Picture, the whole room became aligned. You knew what my intent was—my Future Picture—and all I did was add a unifying strategy: *Lean in "this" direction*. After that, it was up to you to tactically execute any way you saw fit. I offered no techniques, no tactical guidance. You chose to put out your left hand and you chose to push to the left and suddenly, this whole room was executing strategically."

Strategy. Not tactics.

STRATEGY VERSUS TACTICS

As I said at the beginning of this chapter, few people define strategy the same way, so let's get the Flawless Execution definition of *strategy* on the table. Strategy, quite simply, is asking four very important things:

1. *Where* are we going to be in the future?
2. *What* are we going to apply our resources into or against in order to get there?
3. *How* are we going to do this?
4. And *when* or how are we going to exit or get out—how do we *finish with finesse?*

Let's look at Vietnam. For the sake of this illustration, let's say that we had more than 1,000 engagements with the Viet Cong in our quest to win the war. Maybe it was more, maybe less; the number's unimportant. The fact is this—we won about 90 percent of the battles. Ninety percent! Our tactics were superior, our equipment was superior; our aircraft, our weapons, our soldiers, and our training were superior. So, battle by battle, we won more than we lost. Tactically, we won by a decisive margin, but, strategically, we were humbled and humiliated. In the end, our mighty military, with all of its superior technology and all of its training, was forced to use that technology and training to do little more than evacuate Saigon from the rooftop of the United States Embassy Building as Saigon became Ho Chi Minh City.

Tactically, we won. Strategically, we lost.

Tactics are rarely decisive. When competition is based on tactics alone, the tactics rapidly lose their effectiveness. Examples? Forward air controllers directed the air strike missions in Vietnam. These were guys in small airplanes with propeller-driven engines. They scanned the brush for targets. When they had a target, they called in the jets. Over time, guess what? The enemy adjusted and when they heard the sound of that small propeller engine, they simple moved. When our fire-breathing, heavy metal, F-4 Phantoms came in to take out a target, they did an extraordinarily good job of blowing up dirt.

Tactics lose their effectiveness in a short amount of time. Said differently, tactics are almost always short-term fixes. A company watches the sales of its products slip. It institutes a price promotion, let's say a 30-percent-off weekend special. Sales jump up, don't they? But, in a week or so, sales turn downward again. Tactics.

Let's look at something that appears to be strategic but on further examination is yet another tactic. In the fast food industry, restaurants that embraced drive-thru windows showed a sharp increase in business but, in short order, the drive-thru concept was commonplace. At first blush, it seemed strategic, but in fact it was tactical. The early adopters had a temporary advantage, but in time, competitors copied the concept, sales fell back to their historical levels, customers returned to their patterns, and the drive-thru window is now . . . just there.

Tactics are basic actions of an organization. Tactics are promotions, discounts, temporary price reductions, gifts-with-purchase. Tactics don't guarantee success. Equally, success doesn't require superior tactics. America's superior firepower and technology didn't guarantee success on the Vietnam battlefield.

Now let's look at a strategy. Apple had a superior computer, but they refused to license the operating system. The PC came along and Microsoft initiated an open-licensing strategy. In a few years, Microsoft OS–powered PCs dominated the market. Despite everything marketing theory teaches you, Apple, one of the best, most user-friendly computers on the market ended up with just a miniscule share of a marketplace they helped define. Apple had a poor strategy; Microsoft had a winning strategy.

What accounts for this counterintuitive result? History teaches us that in both business and war it is strategy that makes the difference. In Vietnam, the United States had a poor strategy. No matter how hard our guys fought, it made little difference to the outcome. North Vietnam had a "good enough" strategy. "Foreigners will not occupy our country," they said. "We will wear the Americans down and be happy so long as we're moving toward Saigon."

The lesson is this: Good strategy can allow you to succeed even with inferior products or tactics.

Alternatively, trying to win by pouring more money and more energy into tactics rarely results in a decisive or permanent victory. Price cuts are matched by competitors; the consumer gets numb to promotions.

CREATING STRATEGY

As we stated earlier in the chapter, there are four essential elements to creating winning strategies. The first is familiar to you. *Where?* Where do you want to be in the future? Strategies start with the Future Picture.

The second question is *What?* What are you going to apply your resources into or against in order to achieve your Future Picture?

The third is *How?* How are you going to apply your resources?

The fourth is deciding ahead of time when you will finish or *finish with finesse.*

So, where does one start? We call it mapping the system and identifying the centers of gravity—the system's centers of gravity, which, as you will learn, are key to building strategy.

MAPPING SYSTEMS

As we mentioned earlier in the book, everything exists inside a system. At a very basic level, your body is a system. Your lungs take in oxygen, your heart distributes it, your liver cleans your blood, and so on.

A car requires an engine, tires, steering mechanism, and brakes to work, or the "system," called a car, breaks down. The U.S. government operates as a system; Wal-Mart is a system.

The point is, everything operates as a system.

A key concept to developing strategy is to understand that systems resist change. Look at what is called the Hysteresis Effect. When you jump on a diving board it bends but then springs back to its original position. Bend a pencil and when you release the pressure it returns to what it was before. If a virus enters our body, white blood cells go into action and fight it back. Systems resist change. Ask any IT executive what it is like to roll out a new computer software system to her company and she will definitely tell you that systems resist change!

Now, if all systems resist change, how do you put a system in a new state of energy? If I bend that pencil a little more it will break, and when it does it has permanently entered a new energy (and physical) state. We change a system by applying energy at the right points to cause the system to "break." We change it according to our Future Picture. To achieve your Future Picture you inevitably must break the elastic barriers of the "old" system and put the system in a new energy state. You create a new system— one that benefits you.

If everything operates as a system, and systems resist change, the only way we can change a system is by mapping it out and finding those points where, when sufficient energy is applied, the system changes in accordance with our Future Picture.

Mapping the system is that process. The key to changing a

system is to understand how things relate, how things move, communicate, and interact. The key to understanding that is to map the system out. Let's look at a business. Businesses operate as systems. They have elements that are external and internal. What are in those elements? Externally, there are competitors, consumers, retailers, distributors, and consumer perception. External elements of a business' system include the competition's leadership, the capital markets, media, regulators, and other industries that may influence yours. To write strategy you map out the external system, eliminating nothing that touches or affects you or your company, however odd or seemingly irrelevant it may seem.

In order to effect change on an external system you must also change your internal system. Walt Disney had a Future Picture of the amusement park industry. In his picture, he saw a place where Americans would stay for as long as a week. They would check into a wonderful, fun hotel; eat delicious meals; and be entertained by some of the most imaginative rides in the world.

It was heresy. In the 1950s, amusement parks were seedy, the rides were predictable, the food little more than cotton candy, hot dogs, and popcorn. Stay at the park? For a *week?* People went to amusement parks for the day. Disney not only had to map out the external system he would need to effect in order to realize his Future Picture, but more importantly, he needed an entirely new internal system to pull it off. He needed an internal system that handled customer interactions, transportation, lodging, and food service and maintained the now world-famous Disney *experience.*

Internal systems include your CEO, board members, executives, employee groups, communications infrastructure, buildings, marketing collateral—all of your internal resources. In order to see how everything relates with one another, you must map out that system. Eliminate nothing. Include everything.

Now, looking at your internal and external systems, you're ready to learn a huge amount of information on the interrelated

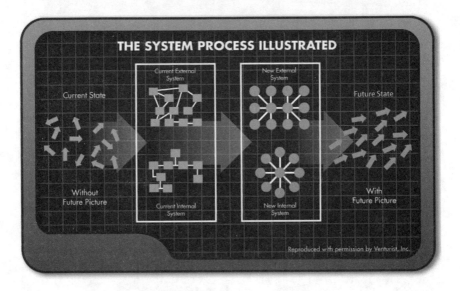

elements that make up these systems. Herein lies a problem. Once you've mapped out your system, you will quickly see that there are far too many elements or "nodes" than you have resources to effect. But are there? In truth, some nodes will give you more bang for the buck than others. By going through this mapping process you will be able to identify centers of gravity.

CENTERS OF GRAVITY

Centers of gravity are those critical leverage points where, if pressure is applied, your resources gain the most impact on that system. Wal-Mart wanted to become the dominant retailer but didn't see any percentage in opening up thousands of small stores and just blending into the retail landscape. They saw *huge*, big box stores as a way to change the landscape. This was their center of gravity. They could change the system; they would make people come to their stores, but by having huge stores filled with big quantities of everyday products priced below competition. The age of mom-and-pop retailing effectively ended.

If you believe that everything operates in a system and systems have centers of gravity, you can change a system by changing its center of gravity.

TARGETING

Once you've identified your centers of gravity, you have a related question: *What do I do now?* Most companies would rank or order their priorities and then go after each, one by one, until the budget runs out or the tasks are completed. We call this *attacking in serial.* History shows us that prolonged, serial warfare leads only to a protracted battle. Ultimately, the longer the battle, the worse the odds become to achieve your Future Picture. Why? As time goes on the system begins to counterattack. It begins to defend itself and, with time, it gets better and better at defending itself, defeating your Future Picture. As time goes on, the cost of operations increases. It is far better to attack your centers of gravity in parallel—rapidly, all at once. You shock the system and put it in a new energy state.

Colonel John Warden did this brilliantly during Desert Storm. Let's look at it.

During the Gulf War, the Future Picture was to get Saddam out of Kuwait. One of the elements in that picture was to minimize collateral damage. The planners mapped out the external system of Iraq, which included over 300,000 targets! It was too many to deal with, so they identified centers of gravity, things like command posts and radar sites. Among these centers of gravity was the Iraqi electrical system. The electrical system had many components—hundreds if not thousands of them—with the obvious ones being the power-generating plants. If our bombers could take out their power plants, we could deny electricity to the enemy, which in turn would blind his command-and-control facilities and thus reduce his combat effectiveness.

But what constitutes "taking out his power plants"? In the past, from World War II through Vietnam, the conventional thinking was to task heavy bombers like B-52s to a prolonged saturation-bombing campaign. After a few hundred strikes over a period of weeks, after dropping more than a few thousand bombs, the lights in Baghdad would go out.

Warden looked at the "system" and came up with a radically different approach.

"Why destroy the power plants?" he asked. "Is that the leverage point? Does that best achieve the Future Picture?" No. Too many resources would be diverted, the attacks would be serial, the process would take too long, and power could be shunted from one grid to another.

One planner had a better idea. "We can achieve the same results," he argued, "by destroying the step-up transformers—the points where the power aggregates and is then redistributed. Instead of darkening the skies with dozens of bombers for a period of weeks, why not use our smart bombs and our tactical fighter aircraft and, in parallel, take out all of these transformers?" Ever so slowly, the idea gained traction. Soon it became a strategy— use F-15Es and F-111Fs to surgically remove the transformers in a coordinated strike that could be executed in parallel. Do it quickly, from one end of the country to the other. The desired outcome would be achieved—the lights would go out in Baghdad; the enemy would be blinded and collateral damage would be held to a minimum. So, in flew the surgical strike teams; and in the first six minutes of the war, out went the lights! (Later, when the bomb damage assessment photographs made their way to the Pentagon, they saw pictures of perfectly intact power plants. Those not in the loop were aghast. "The power plants are up!" they said. Which, of course, is a tactical way of thinking. "Yes, but the lights are out in Iraq," said the strategically aligned field commanders.)

The step-up transformers were centers of gravity within the electrical system that, when broken, altered the system. By hitting these centers of gravity in parallel, the Future Picture was advanced and resources were economized.

The surgical strikes made the system change. It achieved the desired outcome and was consistent with the Future Picture.

When translating the Future Picture into strategies, the answer to *What?* is to identify the place or places within the system that, if attacked, efficiently and effectively change the system in a fashion that helps us achieve our Future Picture. We attack centers of gravity in parallel.

But how does this work in business? Apple's iPod is a marvelous example of mapping out a complex internal and external system then attacking the centers of gravity. Apple quite correctly saw the need for a device that digitally stored songs and allowed users to take those songs with them; they created the digital jukebox. The jukebox was a nifty device, but the sales were poor. Apple pulled back the lens and looked at the system. They mapped out their internal system and then the external system and started to sift through them to identify the centers of gravity. First, they noticed design. Was this product an "Apple product"? Did it look and feel like things Apple designed? They thought not.

Then they looked at the music industry. The music industry, they agreed, was part of the jukebox system—but what a mess it was. Millions of kids were downloading music through illegal websites like Napster, causing the record companies to respond with hundreds of lawsuits. The Internet, in the eyes of the record industry, was a dark force destroying their business. Only a fool would think that the music industry would be a part of this product's success—a product that downloaded music from the Internet.

But Apple saw it as a center of gravity. Without songs, who needed a digital jukebox? Desired effect? What if they could convince the industry to license their songs to a secure, Apple-controlled, fee-based website that could turn pirated digital music into a new revenue stream for the record industry? What if they could "break" an external system that resisted downloadable digital music and make it work for Apple?

So, Apple worked with the record industry, wrangled download rights to tens of thousands of songs and created an Internet store called iTunes. They found an attractive price-per-download and agreed to a shared revenue model.

In parallel, they attacked their second center of gravity—design. They redesigned the jukebox and renamed the sleek new device the iPod. And they did this all in less than nine months, a classic outcome of a systems approach and attacking in parallel.

Taken together, attacking these centers of gravity in parallel, they changed the system to their Future Picture—a nation of men, women, and children carrying a small device that stored thousands of songs, with revenue coming not just from the sale of the product but from the sale of the music, too. Neither pioneer nor market share leader at the time, Apple's strategies paid off; today, they have 70 percent of a thriving market.

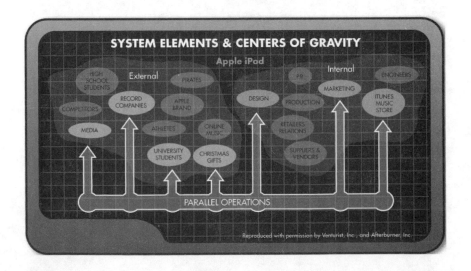

Yes, Apple could have rolled out price cuts and given their re-tailers special incentives to stock more jukeboxes, but those were short-term tactics, and in the end the elements of the system would resist change.

The folks at Apple mapped out the system, identified centers of gravity, and then attacked in parallel. And they were smart enough and their product was hip enough to pull it off. The iPod is now nothing less than a cultural phenomenon. iTunes has more than one million songs available for download. Hewlett-Packard has even launched an official, licensed version of the iPod. The institutional memory at Apple recalled the disaster of the deci-sion way back when not to license their operating system, and did not allow the company to make the same mistake twice.

CHAPTER 6 ▶▶▶▶▶ ✈ ▶▶▶▶▶▶▶▶▶▶▶▶

Leader's Intent

It is not enough to just know the strategy . . .
but the decisions behind the strategy.

Reproduced with permission by Afterburner, Inc.

The astute reader may at this point realize that two things are missing. By what process do you map out systems? And how do we measure our progress against that Future Picture, or our desired effects?

OPEN PLANNING

Against the entire body of prevailing thought in corporate America, we know that planning should be conducted as an open process involving everyone necessary to achieve the Future Picture. Manufacturing, packaging, sales, promotions, advertising, distribution, warehousing, finance, human resources, and any other department charged with executing the Future Picture—these people must be involved in the planning process. They must physically be in attendance and they need to contribute from the beginning. They need to understand the nuances of the Future Picture, contribute to the key descriptors, help map out the system, help identify the centers of gravity (and their desired effects then with vigor and wholehearted buy-in), take this Future Picture back to their teams, and clearly communicate their intent—what we call the *leader's intent*—and allow their team to begin the Plan-Brief-Execute-Debrief-Win cycle that is the hallmark of Flawless Execution.

To some companies this is heresy. Plans come down from the ivory tower, don't they? You have an executive vice president of planning who has a floor filled with MBAs who specialize in planning, who specialize in developing brilliant strategies (notwithstanding the fact that they may never have walked a factory floor or sat down with a buyer for a grocery chain).

In other companies, it's a closed-door affair. The brand manager works on the marketing plan. The manufacturing people work on the production plans. The sales force works on its plans. And nobody tells each other what they're doing.

In truth, both systems fall short. Instead, bring everyone together. Plan in the open. And then watch the results. Open planning is conducive to the vital attributes that are the stock-in-trade of winning companies. Speed to market. Creativity. Collaboration. Opening planning lets everyone see the cause and effects of ideas in real time across all of the departments. Moreover, open planning triggers intense, passionate, and unspeakably valuable buy-in by the people who will have to put the plan into effect; for, in the end, nothing defeats a plan faster than apathetic, grumbling, reluctant executors. By being there and knowing everyone's intent, everyone can make decisions at the field level, confident that they are making the right decisions since they were present when the decisions behind the development of the strategy were made.

Who uses open planning? In forty-eight hours, the Department of Defense wrote the war plan for Operation Desert Storm. To accomplish this incredible feat, Colonel John Warden demanded the attendance of a representative from every support asset in the military—over 200 people in all—and assembled them in the basement of the Pentagon in a room called Checkmate. They walked out with the strategies that would achieve the president's overall Future Picture and win a war in 100 days. Centers of gravity were identified and targeted, and measures of this future success were established.

Some rules of thumb:

- **Open planning.** The environment must be conducive to ideas. People in the process should check their egos at the door. Open planning takes open minds.
- **No tactics.** Because the goal is to determine the future as your team wants it to be, tactics are not on the agenda. Deal with them later, not here. To give but one example of the difference, in the example of the new product a company is about to introduce, mass media may be the best advertising strategy, but whether to advertise on NBC or CBS is tactical. Tactical discussions are not welcome.
- **Be quick about it.** The planning process should be dynamic and time-compressed. The best thinking is done when your

backs are against the wall. Deadlines should be measured in hours and the process in just days. Remember—Desert Storm was planned in forty-eight hours.

- **Everyone contributes.** Everybody speaks and everyone contributes. This forges a valuable interaction. Vital contributions may come from the least expected corners. Leaders who rarely collaborate find themselves mixing concepts with people they hardly know, thus creating entirely new points of view. Everyone contributes to the Future Picture. Everyone contributes to the key descriptors. And everyone writes the measures of merit.

CAMPAIGN ROOMS

The planners of Desert Storm configured Checkmate in a very effective way. The room was large enough to support 200 people. In the middle of the room was the commander's table, where the leaders could see the action unfolding around them. Each campaign team or mission team owned a section of the wall on which was pasted block paper notes, planning docs, maps, and intelligence pictures. As new people entered the room, they could walk around the perimeter and quickly get up to speed on the current state of the overall plan as well as the many centers of gravity and their variables.

Can this work in business? The BAMA Company sells pastries to fast food restaurants such as McDonalds. To achieve their productivity and quality goals they use this process. BAMA rented a semi-trailer and put it smack in the middle of their factory parking lot. This became the BAMA campaign room. Displayed on the walls are the twelve key descriptors and measures of merit. Every time a new employee comes online, he or she is required to take a lap around the campaign trailer, read the Future Picture, and understand the company's strategy. The leader's intent at BAMA is at work in the campaign room getting the newest arrow aligned. The effectiveness has flowed over to the employees' families; the trailer has become a way they show off their pride in BAMA and the great work everyone has done. The results have been spectacular. Since adopting open planning, BAMA has won the prestigious Malcolm Baldrige Award and continues to grow its business. Open planning is the key to the leader's intent being executed throughout the ranks of the organization.

FINISHING WITH FINESSE

The last aspect of developing strategy is answering the very important question of when or how are we going to exit? The two most vulnerable times in a company's life are at the beginning and at the end. Generally speaking, entrepreneurs put enormous amounts of time into planning the start-up but very little into planning the exit strategy. A typical business plan may have twenty pages explaining the business and how it will compete, but just one page on the exit strategy. Why don't companies and individuals put the same amount of energy into the end—after all, everything ends, right? Few wars end in good peace and few companies or products end on a high note.

Look at the following figure of the typical life cycle of a product or service. In the beginning, buckets of resources and energy are expended to get this product above the black line into profitability. The marketing and sales departments ramp up and embrace this hot new item. Profits soar and the company invests even more resources to scale the product. Things look great; life is good.

But eventually the product reaches a point where sales flatten, maybe level off, and profits dip. What happens? A call goes out from the CEO to make the changes necessary to keep the mo-

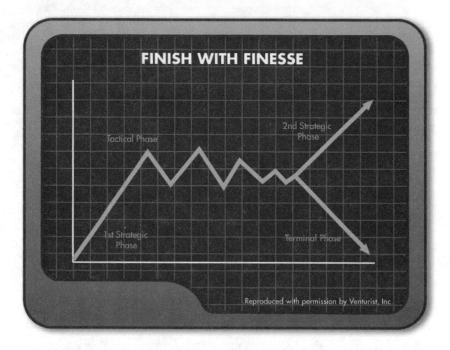

mentum going: Hire a new marketing head, reenergize the sales force, institute six sigma into the manufacturing department. Promotions. Specials. Deals. Profits rise again, but soon the gradual plunge returns.

The company is now riddled with angst. Management is trying to put its arms around air. The company spends and spends but nothing happens except that it slides further down until it's out of cash and maybe out of business. What's wrong? It has no measures of merit to guide it through the inevitable point where a product wears out. The company hasn't planned its exit strategy. It hasn't written into its business plan the milestones that, when reached, trigger an appropriate exit strategy.

Look at companies that do plan their exit strategies. Hollywood, for one, is superb at this. Movies have distinct sales patterns, and the studios track indicators like a hawk. The first indicator is the weekend gross when the movie opens at the movie theaters. This is a critical benchmark. Let's say the movie opens nationwide with $40 million in grosses. Right away the studio has a rough idea if the movie will become profitable. Now they wait for the second week's grosses. Grosses almost always decline. The first week will be the best week; the question is, how good are its legs? Week number two starts to tell the story. If the grosses decline less than twenty per cent, the movie's hot and has good legs. If the grosses plunge, the measures of merit tell the studio to pull the plug. Cut back on the advertising. The movie has done what it can. Get ready to put money behind the next release. Push up the home video release date.

That's how studios think. From the moment they release a movie, they're in the finish-with-finesse portion of their business plan. From the moment the movie hits the theaters, the studio is in the exit strategy phase of the product's life cycle.

Coca-Cola is another company that understands life cycles. Coca-Cola expects its product life cycle to be in multiples of generations, not merely years or weeks, so it has its own measures of merit. How do we keep Coke relevant, corporate honchos ask? People change, tastes mature. How does Coke maintain market share and profitability as the consumer shifts? At some point the company will introduce a line extension. Line extensions adapt a product to trends in the marketplace, which in turn keeps the brand relevant. What are brand extensions? Diet Coke. Lime Coke. Vanilla Coke. Cherry Coke. And now C2—the low-carb Coke.

The point is this: Know where you are in your product's life cycle and plan on exiting with finesse. Generally, that leaves you with two choices. You can wind up and dissolve the company like a movie studio treats a movie, or you can embark on a new strategy like Coke does. When you embark on a new strategy you are exiting the old plan with finesse. An easy example of this comes from the hotel industry. Believe it or not, in the mid-1960s, it was rare for a resort hotel to have a golf course. But consumers were changing; they wanted more recreational amenities. New hotels started to be built with great golf courses around their properties so the old hotels had to make a strategic adjustment. They added golf courses and upped the room rate. That's exiting the old business—hospitality—with finesse. The resort hotels become golf resorts.

Passenger shipping lines have been adept at this. The old idea of a five-day cruise across the ocean has been replaced by countless new ideas. Weekend cruises to nowhere. Cruises packed with energetic, active land excursions. The shipping lines finished with finesse. Nowadays, they are hardly in the business of a quiet Atlantic crossing.

You are going to come to the end of your mission. In that there is no doubt. Why not determine how you will finish ahead of time so you and your employees finish with finesse? Sound strategies are built on finishing with finesse.

All of this goes into the open planning process and comes out in the end as a package—the Future Picture, the key descriptors, the measures of merit, centers of gravity, their desired effects, and the exit points. Since the leaders were part of this process through open planning, they are carrying a package they understand and "own," which can then be effectively delivered to the

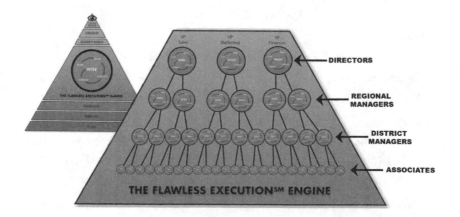

team. The leader can lay out the picture in detail, and, in turn, create a clear statement of his own Future Picture for his department, or the center(s) of gravity his team must effect. This in turn directs the actions of the tactical team, guided by the intent of their leader. From this point forward, the team goes into the Plan-Brief-Execute-Debrief-Win cycle.

Here in the execution engine, the Flawless Execution cycles begin to spin.

The Flawless Execution Engine

To win in a dynamic environment you must accelerate
the experience of your team.

Reproduced with permission by Afterburner, Inc.

Up to now, we've been dealing with broad, generalized statements. *Future Picture*: A picture of the future as you want it to be.
Strategies: High-value centers of gravity executed in parallel that

focus resources on the key leverage points to achieve the Future Picture.

Now we're in the execution engine, the place where we bring the strategy down to the squadrons and actually fly our mission. Here is where we are dealing with tactics—the daily execution, the job of putting the bombs on the targets, missiles on Migs, products on shelves, closing sales, and inching ourselves one step forward toward the Future Picture. Here is where we break down the general picture and translate it into specifics.

Here the rules change.

Let's review where we are. The first three sections in the Flawless Execution Model were designed to be general and far ranging, open to creativity without getting bogged down with tactics. No longer. Now we're getting to specifics. Did we take out the SAM site? Did we take out the bridge north of Baghdad? Did we finish installing the new software? Outcomes are now vitally important and detail is everything. Down in the tactical teams, our objectives are specific, clear, measurable, and achievable and developed down to the smallest detail. Everything we ask our people to do is contributing to the overall Future Picture.

Another change: In the introduction I talked about latitude. So far, the word has been irrelevant. In developing the Future Picture and mapping out the system, there is no need for constraints; therefore, there was not a need to introduce latitude.

Now latitude will enter the picture. Everyone on the team will not only have a measurable, quantifiable objective, but in executing their mission, they will be given a clear understanding of what the leader's intent is so they have latitude to adapt to changing conditions.

EXECUTING THE COMMANDER'S INTENT

If I'm on the way into a kill box to attack a specific ground-based target (antiaircraft artillery or triple-A site) and I notice another group of targets similar in nature and posture to the ones our mission is targeting, I can divert some of our bombs into this new target, based on my assessment of the assets we are currently carrying. Then I can proceed to the primary target.

Are these tactics written into my mission objective? No. But because I have latitude, each of these "changes" helps realize the overall Future Picture and therefore they are good. Because I understand the commander's intent, which is to eliminate *all* surface-to-air threats in our kill box, and because I have the tools, I have the latitude to flex my attack plan. By taking out another triple-A site, I contribute to the overall objective.

Everyone needs latitude, but the degree of latitude will progressively narrow as one gets closer to the place where we execute. I liken it to superhighways and roads. A CEO or an entrepreneur has complete latitude; the service clerk at McDonald's has a narrow goat path. Media buyers in the media department may substitute radio for part of the TV schedule but not change the product being advertised. They have that latitude because they understand the intent of their mission (saturation advertising for three weeks, let's say) and how it supports the commander's intent (successfully launch a new product).

In the execution engine, we're dealing with action. We've gone from the big picture to combat. Whether I'm sitting strip alert in my F-15 guarding our borders or flying a dawn mission over Baghdad, I'm living and breathing inside the world of execution; how well I do is a matter of life or death.

There's a proven process that leads to flawless execution—the Plan-Brief-Execute-Debrief-Win cycle. It's a time-tested process that keeps fighter pilots winning, that gets us to our targets and brings us back home with a success under our belts. We've seen it work in Desert Storm and Afghanistan and in thousands of businesses.

Here are the essential elements.
The Plan-Brief-Execute-Debrief-Win Cycle

Once the leader has communicated the Future Picture and the package of key descriptors, centers of gravity, and their desired effects, the tactical teams enter into a tactical planning phase to translate the strategy into specific, tactical missions. These missions will be responsible for the desired effect of a particular center of gravity. This process has only four steps: plan-brief-execute-debrief.

Plan

Before we do anything, we thoroughly plan the mission. To do that, we have a specific process we call the Six Steps to Mission Planning. The Six Steps are where the field commander or field representative takes the intent based on the Future Picture and strategy, and focuses it into a very specific tactical plan—a plan that accomplishes the desired effect or end state for a particular center of gravity. This person was present in the open planning process and thus knows not only the strategy but the decisions behind the strategy. Since he comes from one of the departments and thus is intimately familiar with the tactical environment for the team, the planning and ensuing tactics are aligned with the strategy.

Brief

Once we have the plan, we brief that plan to all of the mission participants. To ensure that no one involved has any questions as to what is expected from him or her, or, more importantly, any questions as to how our plan will be executed, briefings take place right before our teams execute.

Execute

Armed with our brief, we execute the mission like an actor speaking memorized lines and practiced moves in a play. We know where we are going, where we've been, where we are, and what we're going to do next, down to the second. To maintain that high level of awareness, which we call *situational awareness*, we employ specific tools to keep us ahead of the silent killer of execution—task saturation.

Debrief

Our most important, enduring, institutional step in this four-step process is the after-mission debrief. In my old business, after every mission, every participant walked directly from their jets to the debriefing room, and in it they examined their execution down to the finest detail. They were looking for ways to improve their performance. Debriefing is done in a nameless and rankless environment, using a specific process called STEALTH, which forces your organization to freely admit and examine errors or acknowledge successes. The STEALTH process makes certain that lessons learned are then funneled back into tomorrow's mission to make it tighter; if we have a lesson that's big enough, we communicate it throughout the whole organization to accelerate everyone's experience.

Win

No sooner have we debriefed one mission than we start another. Whether you flew a good mission or a sloppy one, you're alive and you have to get ready for the next. You may have a sales trip planned for the next day or you may have a family vacation. No matter what, you apply the Flawless Execution Model to every situation in life. So remember this—after the debrief, after the moment when you return, you start planning for the next mission. That's the secret to Flawless Execution. You never leave the Flawless Execution cycle. You just move from one mission to another. You move from one Flawless Execution cycle to another.

This is the heart of the Flawless Execution Model: Plan. Brief. Execute. Debrief. Win.

It begins with the plan.

CHAPTER 8 ▶▶▶▶▶▶▶✈▶▶▶▶▶▶▶▶▶▶

Planning

Flexibility is the key to airpower . . .
preparation is the key to flexibility.

THE SIX STEPS TO MISSION PLANNING

Mission planning is not hard but it is *thorough*. Our way of planning calls for a resolution of detail that most people have never considered. It's no different from the detail we painted in the Future Picture. We fill the canvas with detail and with color.

First, a perspective. Tactical planning allows us to project our thoughts forward in time and space and allows us to influence events before they occur rather than reacting to events as they occur. We are attempting to influence our destiny by being proactive, instead of allowing someone or something to determine the outcome.

Then consider this: Tactical planning forms a disciplined framework for approaching problems. It gives us multiple courses of actions, an opportunity to evaluate them, then the chance to take the best pieces from each and create the best plan. With our enhanced understanding of potential outcomes, we can better prepare to make time-critical decisions and have resources at hand.

In short, it brings us into the cycle of Flawless Execution.

Fighter pilots hate surprises. It's hard enough hanging on to a jet while it's flying through the air at 700 miles per hour and putting nine bone-crushing Gs on you. It's enough to monitor your instruments, work the radar, listen to the calls on the radio, and dodge an extremely hostile enemy. The last thing you want to do is figure out a solution that requires more than a fraction of a second of thought. There's no time for complexity in the air while a pilot is executing his mission. The time for thinking is on the ground. That's why pre-mission planning is *thorough*. Yours will be, too.

To cover all the bases, we break the planning process down into six steps. Whether you're a fighter pilot or a businessperson, *you must go through these six steps before you have a plan*. Have we *really* covered all the bases? Are we *really* ready for that important meeting? The only way to know is to tick off the six steps one by one.

The Six Steps to Mission Planning
- **Step One:** Determine the Mission Objective
- **Step Two:** Identify the Threats
- **Step Three:** Identify Your Available Resources
- **Step Four:** Evaluate the Lessons Learned
- **Step Five:** Determine Courses of Action/Tactics
- **Step Six:** Plan for Contingencies

STEP ONE: DETERMINE THE MISSION OBJECTIVE

A mission objective is not the Future Picture nor is it the desired effect of a center of gravity. A mission objective is something that you and I can go out and execute today, in today's mission. A good mission objective has to be clear. It must be measurable (quantifiable). It must be achievable (believable). And it must support the overall Future Picture of the organization.

Let's look at each criterion. First, the objective has to be clear. A good mission objective uses ordinary, simple language. For example, you may be tempted to use lingo or slang, but don't; your job is to be *understood*. Too many corporate executives like to sprinkle in hip new business words that are colloquial or trendy but not readily understood. If your people don't know what you mean—or worse, if your words are subject to differing interpretations—you're in trouble, and that certainly means the mission is in trouble, too.

A mission objective is clear, specific, and easily understood by all.

Second, the objective must be measurable. Did we take out the SAM site? In the cold light of day, our battle damage assessment photography will tell us exactly how well we did. A mission objective is measurable on some quantifiable scale. Here's a good objective: "We will destroy Al-Qaeda's C3i (command, control, and communications facility; i.e., headquarters building) by 0905z. I know where the C3i is located, and through proper intelligence I understand the structure of the building and its foundation, which will be matched with the proper size and configuration of bomb we will carry. In turn I know that if we hit the target, we will destroy it. And I realize we must do this in a very coordinated and timely manner since intelligence has told us that high-level Al-Qaeda officials will be present at 0905z.

By contrast, a weak mission objective might be this: "We will take out Al-Qaeda SAM sites in today's mission." What does that mean? How do we measure the phrase "take out"? Does that mean that we were successful if we hit the tracking radar unit of this site but not the linked missile silos? What if we "take out" the target but the SAM site is back up in an hour? And how many sites does "sites" represent? Three? Five?

I understand what it means to *destroy* a SAM site. I understand what it means to close eight sales or to put exactly twenty-four qualified leads into my sales funnel. But I don't understand what it means to "take out" a SAM site or to "load up the pipeline and pump 'em out the other side." The objective must be measurable.

Next, the objective must be achievable, that is, believable or obtainable. How many times have you been given a mission objective that was brilliant but there was no way you could accomplish it? I guarantee you, if you're going to risk men's and women's lives, that mission objective better be achievable and believable. That doesn't mean it has to be easy. On the contrary: Tough missions are worthy challenges. But it *does* mean that it has to be within the realm of possibility. I can't grow corn in a week or build a factory in five days. It has to be attainable.

The same holds true for business. If you're going to put people into motion, nothing degrades their abilities, their motivation, their energy, or their enthusiasm faster than to give them an impossible task. It just doesn't work. You *can* ask them to stretch. They *can* do whatever it takes: work brutal hours, travel on a weekend, use all of their time, talent, and treasures. But if what you ask is impossible, there is simply no chance for success.

Finally, a mission objective must support the overall Future Picture of the organization. If I'm going to risk my life, I'd like to know how. If, for example, I were an F-117 fighter pilot, and my mission will affect the Future Picture, I want to know it *mattered*. A good mission objective for me might not only be to destroy the target but to destroy a *valuable* target. Destroy Al Qaeda's C3i—their command, control, communication, and intelligence facility—by 0905z. That's a mission objective. The objective is crystal clear. It's measurable. Either I hit the C3i or I don't. With the jet I fly, it's attainable, believable, and achievable. Moreover, I'm motivated. It's an important target. I understand how taking out the nerve center—their command, control, communication, and intelligence facility—will help accomplish the overall Future Picture of the organization: winning the war.

Give me a mission objective well suited to my skills, well

suited to my assets, and in line with my commander's intent, and I'm willing to risk my life. That's what I'm trained to do. It's my type of mission, one with a quantifiable measure of my success, one that contributes to the overall Future Picture of the organization. I'm *ready* to go. Not just ready—I'm *eager* to go. I *want* to get airborne, face the potential SAM and triple A threats, and get over the target because I *want* to destroy that objective. If it puts me and my jet in harm's way, well, that's what it takes. I'm in.

Does your mission objective get past those vertical head nods and reach down to the hidden part in all of us where we execute with passion? Fighter pilots are out there in a hostile environment, flying at 700 miles per hour, risking their lives, yet doing it with passion. Don't you want to feel that passion? Don't you want your people to execute with passion? I promise you, it's possible. An achievable mission turns a salesperson into a superstar. Have you ever read how intense Ted Turner was when he was young and selling advertising for his TV station, WTBS? In those early years Turner was so motivated, so passionate about his business that on occasion he would actually end up on top of a client's desk screaming about the virtues of advertising on his TV station. This wasn't a guy giving lip service to a sales quota. This was a man with a mission. That, my friends, is a Leaning-Forward fighter pilot. Passionate about doing it right. Passionate about winning. Empowered with a clear, measurable, achievable objective that supported the overall Future Picture. Sell advertising on WTBS. Build a big company. Get rich.

Just look where Turner is now.

STEP TWO: IDENTIFY THE THREATS

Unlike the strategic phase where we don't focus on tactics, threats stand between our current position and where we want to go, today, tactically. Now we have to figure out what threats stand in the way of our future picture today or in the present tense of our tactical mission objective. Well, really, what's to learn? That there's a new pizza store down the block or that someone is introducing a new bottled water or a competitor has introduced a new insurance package. So what?

If you want to build a foundation to execute flawlessly in any environment—much less the hostile, rapidly changing environment of business—this step is critical; you have to identify and know your threats. As a fighter pilot, I wanted to know everything. I mean, think about it. People were gunning for me, there were SAMs out there to shoot me down; I was risking my life. How well did I want to know my threats? I can tell you, you get real serious about gathering information when your life is on the line.

You have threats on sales calls. You have them on a request for proposals. Someone or something is out there ready to blow you out of the sky. Someone has a new pricing plan that you hadn't heard about or a new $6 electric toothbrush that just put your $20 toothbrush out of business! As Intel's former CEO Andy Grove would say, "Be paranoid." Let them ridicule you for your paranoia. But dig down. Go through the competition's sales catalog. Do some research. Figure out what your threats are.

Internal and External Threats

There are two types of threats you have to consider: the external threats and the internal threats. In my F-15, an external threat was the Mig-29. I wanted to know everything about that threat that I could learn. This went beyond the make and model of the jet my adversary flew; I wanted to get into his head. For example, as an F-15 fighter pilot, my job was to provide air superiority over the battlefield. I wanted to know everything about the Mig-29, for example. Tell me its top speed, maximum altitude, type of armament, speed, range, and so on. But I also wanted to know everything about the man or woman who was flying that aircraft—because, ladies and gentlemen, I bet my life on the information I got when, at 30,000 feet, we merged and went head to head.

I wanted to know what they had for breakfast in the morning.

I wanted to know what their religious beliefs were, their political aspirations, how they were aligned in their economy.

I wanted to know if he or she had a fight with their spouse or was worried about a check bouncing. Do you get it? I wanted to know everything about their training, their background, and their motivation. What was in their heart, what was in their gut, what was in the soul of that person?

The same went for that SAM site and its crew, or any other external threat I faced. I dug down *deep*.

Do you do the same thing before you go on a sales call? Do you know who your counterpart is and what his or her situation is? I hope so. If not, learn it. Go to association meetings, Rotary Club meetings, meet-and-greets. Dig through their website, their product catalogs; listen to their conference calls with analysts; talk to your vendors. Last year I flew to Australia, Hong Kong, and countless other domestic destinations as a part of my organization, YEO—Young Entrepreneurs Organization. I listened. I learned. I saw what motivated my peers, how they were running their companies, and what they thought tomorrow might bring. Was I taking notes? You bet.

Look at the external threat factors but also the personal drivers behind those factors, whether it's the attitude of a company or their Future Picture or their culture or the problems your threat had that morning on the way to the office. You can't be too informed.

You also have to look at internal threats. They are in your own company, within the four walls of your building. One famous general's quote rings true to this: "We have met the enemy and the enemy is us." What are these internal threats? We call them

CIA. *Complacency*, *Indifference*, and *Apathy*. Whether you're in a strong economy or a weak economy, you cannot be complacent about growing or developing new products or going into new markets. Do you think your customers are really satisfied with last year's product? Never. But do they tell you? Do they push you to get out of the box and come up with something radically different? No. Customers don't want change; they like the status quo. They may want a new feature or faster service but rare is the day that they ask for something revolutionary.

Do you get a wake-up call before you're dead in the water? Not likely. You have to fight complacency, indifference, and apathy with the certain knowledge that someone's about to do you one better. In truth, companies that are complacent, indifferent, and apathetic are the ones most vulnerable to innovation. Take disruptive technologies. Disruptive technologies are always over the horizon—but they are there. Wi-Fi is evolving into a wireless broadband product for homes and businesses that completely bypasses the copper lines the telephone companies have spent billions of dollars to put in-ground. That's disruptive. The iPod? Will it disrupt sales at the record stores? Probably. What do you think the future of the video store is with cable systems testing On-Demand TV? The fact is, see them or not, you can count on something being out there ready to tickle the tail of the dragon.

When you look at threats, look at the internal factors as well—communication, proficiency, training, and the personal drivers behind them all. Pfizer is the largest pharmaceutical company in the world. We have worked with them for over seven years. They have seen massive change in their industry—mapping the human genome, mergers, compliance issues, and scandals, to name a few. Recently, I was working with Pfizer Australia and we were in the middle of planning a workshop to ready their marketing and sales teams for a new year of product introductions. They split our planning teams into four major drug areas, such as central nervous system drugs and cardiovascular drugs. Each group was responsible for their respective categories.

Like most industries, the pharmaceutical industry is extremely competitive, so when we started down the path of listing threats, our teams intuitively focused on the competition. To look at their whiteboards you would think that this was the most competitive industry in the world. I said, "Fine, now what about the internal threats?" It took a while, but they finally discovered that the biggest threat they had was not from the outside but from the inside—from a lack of collaboration between marketing and medical. You see, in the pharmaceutical industry research and development scientists work on the next generation of drugs, while medical specialists evaluate the drug trials to ensure the drug is safe and performs as advertised, and the marketing people make certain that the sales department is armed with the proper information, samples, and technical expertise to convince doctors to prescribe the drugs. The problem came up between the medical guys and the marketing guys. The medical guys were science-based and black and white. For the most part they were quiet and hesitant to make any statements or claims until all the evidence was in. The sales and marketing guys were outgoing and action oriented; they would rather die than wait on anything. Medical was not providing marketing with the trial information or timelines required to make marketing plans. The marketing guys wanted to launch today. The medical guys had fundamental and legal obligations to ensure that any information that went out into the field was based on sound scientific research, regardless of marketing's timelines. Encouraging this group to go through the process to identify threats led the group to realize that their own lack of communication and collaboration was much more important than any outside competitor. Pfizer now plans with both teams imbedded with each other, sharing the responsibility of joint mission objectives.

At Afterburner, we ask people to list their internal and external threats, but we also break those threats down to those that are controllable versus those that are uncontrollable. Weather is a good example. Fighter pilots can't control weather, so they highlight it as an uncontrollable threat and deal with it later, in the last step to planning called *contingency planning*.

Finally, prioritize the threats. Which ones pack the most lethality—which ones can do you the most damage? Put them on top of your list. Make certain you understand them, plan for them, and have a resource to deal directly with them. Which leads us into the next step.

STEP THREE: IDENTIFY YOUR AVAILABLE RESOURCES

Now, who or what are your available resources? They are people, money, systems, technologies, products, clients, time, known strengths, services, or skills of the team that help you negate your threats and accomplish your mission objective. Do you have anybody or anything on your team that can help you eliminate or negate those threats? Now, I know what you're thinking out there. You're thinking, "Well, Murph, that's great. I already knew that I've got people on my team or services that can help me." But fighter pilots out there turning and burning, putting missiles on Migs or bombs on target, can't really stop and spend time talking to the maintainer who's turning the wrench on the bottom of that $30 million F-15 they're already flying. Or spend much time with the supply officer in the back office who is supplying us with our G-suit, to help keep oxygenated blood in our heads so we don't pass out when we're pulling nine G's. Or maybe gab with the ground controllers or the AWACs (Airborne Warning and Control). Wanna bet? Fighter pilots know exactly what the maintainer does, what the supply officer with the G-suit does, and how the AWACs are trained and what they can do for him. Fighter pilots know their jobs and how they perform them.

You have to do the same thing in business. You have to know the people in the back office and what they can do for you. Administration, public relations, marketing, manufacturing? These people are resources. Talk to them; listen to what they say. Understand what they do. Ask yourself: How can they help me? You have to walk the manufacturing floor and talk to the factory workers. You have to know what goes in that widget that you're selling. I know it's tough to do but, one day, you're going to be turning and burning, and you're going to wish you had.

Then there are the assets outside your immediate circle of influence. Do you know how to get in touch with that vendor who can help you close the next deal? Have you met the owner of the restaurant who might give you a better table when you're entertaining a client? The devil's in the details. Look at everything and everyone as a potential asset and think about how they might help. Listen to everyone, know how to reach them. Access everything. Look for nuggets of gold everywhere.

If we knew we were going to have a SAM threat, we asked ourselves, what did we have in our inventory list (we call that a "frag" or fragmentary order), today, that we could use to negate that threat? Well, we might have had aircraft performing the Wild Weasel mission on our team that day. These are men and women fighter pilots who leap out of bed every day, looking to hunt and track down surface-to-air missiles. So we knew we had that asset on our playlist today. That's a strength that we had because our Wild Weasels had technology built into their missiles that overcame this particular model of SAMs.

The Voit company was one of the leading manufacturers of volleyballs and soccerballs when the racquetball phenomenon took off. Naturally, as a recreational sports company that made balls, they decided to get into that business, too. Now, Voit wasn't known for racquetballs, but that didn't deter management. They knew how to make great balls and they had distribution in the sporting goods outlets, so they went to work. They designed a ball, came up with attractive packaging, and had a terrific price point—but no one in the company knew how to position their new racquetball versus all the other round balls. It was a tough problem. All racquetballs had to be the same size and weight, and they had to have a specific bounce; those rules were in the federation rule books. So what made one ball different from the other?

The company was stumped. Their New York advertising agency was stumped.

Well, it turns out a salesman was walking through the factory one day when he saw this cannon-like gun firing the new racquetballs against a wall. Bam! Bam! Bam! He asked what was going on. The quality control specialists said they were testing balls to test breakage. Did it all the time, he said.

Breakage! thought the salesman. Breakage was the number one complaint in the industry! So this quick-thinking, Leaning-Forward fighter pilot of a salesman called up the marketing department told them what he saw. The marketing people called their advertising agency and when Voit rolled out their racquetball ads the headline was a winner: "We Fired Our Balls Against a Concrete Wall at 120 Miles per Hour. Guess Who Won?"

Voit became the number one ball in the category.

Once you have listed all of your support assets for the mission, line them up or match them up with possible threats (Post-it notes work well). Do you have enough resources to negate the threats? Do you need all the available resources for the mission at hand? Do you need an ally or an outside source to help? This simple process will give you and your team enormous situational awareness into the potential mission at hand.

Walk the factory floor. There's just no telling where you'll find inspiration, ideas, knowledge, or that one quick fact that closes a sale. Identify your combat-support assets—your team's weapons, your team's people and services—and do this now, in the planning room—*not* in the chaos of battle. Match these assets up with your threats and I guarantee that you will help negate the threat.

STEP FOUR: EVALUATE THE LESSONS LEARNED

Everyone has experiences; someone has been there before. Step four is to tap into those experiences and apply those lessons that fit our mission. Has a team gone before us in a similar situation? Did they make mistakes or did they win big? Wouldn't you like to talk to these individuals before you embark on a similar mission? Did the Wild Weasels take out the SAM site earlier today? Did they have any lessons learned about mobile triple A that was not planned to be in the area but was encountered? If they did have a lesson learned about mobile triple A, we then add it as a planning contingency and adjust our tactics based on this lesson, today! Right now—before we finalize our plan and brief our aircrews.

Has a salesman been to a specific buyer? Does he know the buyer's trigger points? Has someone been to the client's office before? One of my clients rents space in a building that has no parking lot. To make matters worse, his office is next door to a small science museum that seems to be packed with kids. The day I went to introduce myself to him the parking meters were full and the nearest parking lot was ten minutes away. It was a sweltering day, so when I arrived I was a mess. Lesson learned: On the next trip I changed my tactic—I took a cab.

In corporate America, you can't hide the truth and you can't make excuses, not that everyone's got the message. But Merck got it. When an internal study determined that VIOXX, a leading drug for arthritis, might be related to heart attacks, they took the high road and pulled VIOXX off the market entirely. They knew the lessons learned. Tylenol had a potential disaster in the 1980s when someone put poison in some of their bottles. Instead of waiting to see if only a very few bottles were affected, or worse— make excuses or give a public statement about the misfortunes of the terrorist mindset—they immediately removed all of their bottles from the shelves and developed tamper-proof bottles. It is still one of corporate America's great success stories. Tylenol flourished in the aftermath and still dominates its category today. You *never* hide from the truth, *never* cover mistakes with lies.

Lessons learned can be big or little, your experience, the group's experience, or an experience from another company. We search them out write them on the whiteboard, take them apart and feed the mission-critical ones into the planning process.

STEP FIVE: DEVELOP COURSES OF ACTION/TACTICS

At this point your team should be armed with a mission objective, know the threats, have identified the available resources, and have inserted lessons learned. Now it's time to develop a menu of potential courses of action. To do that, we break into small groups and brainstorm ideas. At Afterburner we like a minimum of three groups. Two groups are asked to develop courses of action based on the threats and the available resources, while the third group is allowed to go wild—to develop courses of action assuming a perfect world with unlimited resources.

After about an hour, we merge the groups and, through open planning, look at what we have. For sure, there will be two sets of tactics based on reality and one set of tactics based on an ideal scenario. The two sets of tactics based on reality may be quite different from one another, or they may be similar. Either way, it doesn't matter. We *want* ideas. We *want* creativity. That is why we break up into small groups to ensure that one person or a group of type A's does not control or dominate the brainstorming session. We want everyone's ideas. In fact, the more ideas, the better, because from these three groups we pick the tactics most likely to accomplish our mission. How do we do that?

When we bring the three groups together, we *analyze and finalize* our plan. This requires good facilitation and the ability to put ideas visually in front of the group, usually with whiteboards. Each team lays out its tactics; all of us walk through and pick them apart. It will soon be clear where the strongest elements are for a perfect course(s) of action or tactic based on the collective brainstorming of the group and the work that was done in steps two and three. Once this course(s) of action is decided by your team, we now need to put some accountability around the tactic.

Timing

Once you've decided on the best course(s) of action, it is mandatory to attach a timeline to the mission. *Who* will do *what, when?*

In the world of air combat, the term *decision matrix* is used to describe tactical timelines. A decision matrix puts courses of action on the horizontal line, with hash marks representing decision points. Let's assume we are flying a mission involving four F-15s against a hostile enemy force. We expect to engage these "Bandits" in air-to-air combat. This decision matrix will start sixty nautical miles out from the merge (the point at which we will pass nose to nose on our intercept), with hash marks at forty, thirty, twenty, fifteen, and ten nautical miles. At each hash mark our four-ship of F-15s will perform a series of functions in relationship to the adversaries. For example, at the sixty-miles-to-merge point we will attempt to declare the threat "hostile" and commit our forces. If the threat is flying together we will keep our four ships together in line abreast formation. If we encounter multiple groups or separate formations from the threat, we will counter by splitting our four ships into two groups of two.

At the forty-miles-to-merge point, we will start a climb into thinner air to maximize our missile capabilities and our first launch advantage (missiles aerodynamically perform or shoot farther in the thinner air at high altitude). If the threats are hostile and they meet our shoot criteria, we will ensure that all F-15s are locked on to different targets. At twenty nautical miles our missiles are in the air.

At fifteen miles we will decide whether or not to continue as a four-ship. If at fifteen miles one of us is *spiked* (a term used when an enemy fighter has locked on to you with his radar, indicated by a tone and display in our cockpits), that pilot must break the radar lock and abort by doing a diving 180-degree turn in full afterburner. If you've launched a missile and are not spiked, you will continue to the merge. If you are supporting a missile and you are spiked, you will do a defensive maneuver and attempt to dump the spike. If you are successful, you continue to the merge; if not, abort.

These are our courses of actions laid out on a timeline. This simple timeline enables me to make quick decisions in a mission that will be decided in less than three minutes. Timelines put accountability into the plan. They specify who does what, when. Who will develop what, and when will the marketing collateral materials be finished? If our threat (competitor) launches their fall fashion line before we do, when do we launch our counter campaign? Who will make the call?

Timelines put who, what, and when into the plan. Taken together, the tactics that survived the collective brainstorming of our team are now laid out like a map with an accountability trigger specifying who does what course of action, when. Think you have the perfect plan? We never assume this; before we finalize the course(s) of action, we always "Red Team" the plan.

The Red Team

How would you beat yourself? How would you undermine your sales presentation, defeat the features of your products, turn your price point into a disadvantage, or render your marketing campaign ineffective? During Desert Storm, the planners handed their war plans over to a team that was set up to take it apart and defeat it. Can you imagine that? After all those brilliant, experienced minds came up with the war plan, they gave it to another team and said: "Beat it up. Defeat our plan." What's more, the Red Team had an inside track. They were *not* the enemy. They were not making guesses about timing, tactics, or the performance characteristics of one aircraft or the other. They knew everything.

Beat it they did. Not entirely. But during the Desert Storm planning process the Red Team found weaknesses, weaknesses that would have cost lives in the field. The Red Team made the plans tighter, more foolproof.

Do you have a team ready to take your plan apart and find a way to defeat it? You better, because someone out there is doing just that. Your competition is watching, listening, trying to find out what you're up to. They're going to do all they can to defend their market share, counter your innovations, blunt your marketing attacks, stop your sales growth. How would you defeat yourself? Red Team your plan and then put the surviving courses of action or tactics into action.

STEP SIX: PLAN FOR CONTINGENCIES

We have a saying in the fighter-pilot world: Flexibility is the key to air power.

At Afterburner, we like to take that one step further and say that preparation is the key to flexibility. We spend up to 50 percent of our planning process on step six, asking the very difficult question, "What if?" What if the weather changes over the target area after we launch and get airborne? What if the air refueling tanker does not show up and we can't take on fuel? What if the Wild Weasels cannot take out the SAMs before we get over the target area? Are we going to continue, or are we going to abort the mission? What if? What if? What if?

What about your what-ifs? What if the flight's delayed? What if your PowerPoint presentation locks up? What if the facilitator for your meeting resigned over the weekend? It's much easier if you and I brainstorm these action-item decisions right now, when the winds are calm, in an air-conditioned room, sipping a Coca-Cola instead of two hours later when we're strapped into an F-15, going Mach 1, trying to defeat a surface-to-air missile attack. That's *not* the time to brainstorm. That is the time to execute based on decisions made in the calm comforts of the planning room. There's no time to think things through during the mission. The answers to these questions have to be made in the planning room. This is the time to fine-tune the executional decisions.

Planning for contingencies should be detailed. Start by breaking down your mission into its smallest components, then rank those components on the basis of their importance. What's going to absolutely stop you dead in the water? What one component is the must-have component for the show to go on? Then work out all the ways something can go wrong with that component and what your solutions are. On behalf of our clients, we give seminars in Europe, the Far East, and even Australia. But things change when we go overseas. The customs laws are different, custom offices have different hours, and each country has its own policies about declarations on commercial shipments. In one of our planning meetings, we looked at the what-ifs of giving a seminar overseas. What if our computers were held up in customs? What did we absolutely have to have to give a seminar? In our case, we could do without this or do without that but we absolutely had to have an item we call the *mission planning checklists*. If the carton with the checklists was destroyed, or hung up in customs, or simply lost, what would we do in a foreign country, probably on a Saturday or Sunday when the show had to go on Monday morning in a hotel on a street whose name no one could pronounce? We identified the essential item, loaded it onto our corporate intranet site, gave that area restricted access, and then found a twenty-four-hour office support facility in each city on our travel itinerary. As a backup, we burned a separate copy on a CD-ROM, called it our facilitator emergency CD, and issued this to all our team members.

As it happened, we had to put the plan into action in Portugal when that one-in-a-million series of consecutive mistakes compounded into the worst-case scenario on, of all days, the Sunday before a seminar. Portugal's customs would not release the package that was sent with our seminar materials, due to some holding restrictions unknown to us. Our facilitator had the tools and worked through the night; regardless of how tired he was the next morning, he was in his flight suit and the seminar came off without a hitch.

Without contingency planning, the show would not have gone on. But with *scripted responses*, the precious little time we had was spent executing a solution, not running around like a chicken with its head cut off.

Break your mission apart. Look for the weaknesses. Plan for redundancies. Plan for the redundancy plans to fail. Script your responses. Keep thinking through the what-ifs. I know it sounds like overkill, but bad things happen quickly and without warning.

Once I was in an ACM (Air Combat Maneuvering) engagement, or mock-dogfight, when two jets attacking me rammed into each other. It was a midair collision. Here it was, an ordinary day, and suddenly, two jets had hit each other. That rare, one-in-a-million emergency had struck, but we had a contingency plan, and I had been briefed on this since I started flying fighters. We called it our Midair/Ejection/Rescue section. Do not *under*-fly the last known altitude of the collision. Do not under-fly a parachute. Mark the position of the midair with your INS/GPS (Internal Navigation System/Global Positioning System) for the rescue team. Note the winds aloft (because with strong winds the pilot could drift miles from the midair coordinates).

So what happened on that morning of January 15, at 10:03 A.M., when the midair collision happened? My body and mind went on autopilot. I executed a scripted contingency plan that I never expected to need. Step by step I went through the procedures and helped save the life of a great guy and a great fighter pilot. It was automatic.

Keep peeling back the layers until you don't have anywhere else to go. Once you've got a backup for every item on the must-have list, you're ready to move onto the next phase—execution of your mission.

SUMMARY

Let's look at the six-step process:

- Step one is to determine a mission objective. It's not a Future Picture; it's razor sharp—something that you and I can execute today.
- Step two is to identify the threats—not only external threats, but internal threats as well.
- Step three is to look at your available resources. Look at who and what on your team can help you win.
- Step four is to collect lessons learned from previous missions or the experiences of others that could help you with the mission.
- Step five is to develop your courses of action and Red Team the results.
- Step six is to plan for contingencies.

Use these steps in your planning process and your execution levels will increase significantly.

CHAPTER 9 ▶▶▶▶▶▶▶✈▶▶▶▶▶▶▶▶▶

The Brief

Do not issue marching orders to head for the finish line
until you have told your team where the finish line is . . .

Now, let's talk about how we communicate the plan to the people. We call that the *preflight briefing,* or briefing to win!

You know, it's kind of interesting; we asked a lot of fighter pilots what execution is all about. "Tell me about executing your mission," I said, and each time they gave me this puzzled look and said, "We execute the brief." What they were saying to me was the mission is so tightly tied to the brief that in their minds they didn't know what to talk about except to talk about the brief. That's how important the brief is. In the world of Flawless Execution, *the mission is the brief; the brief is the mission.* The two are inextricably one thing in that pilot's mind, and he or she would no more fly a mission without a brief than drive to work naked.

To a fighter pilot, the brief is such an absolutely critical step in the execution of a mission that we *always* brief every mission, and we do it right before we fly—no exceptions. We don't care if it's a short training flight or a seven-hour combat mission. The brief is where we tell everyone how we're going to carry out the plan and what we're going to do *today.* Everyone's accountable. Every question is covered.

PREPPING FOR THE BRIEFING

So how do fighter pilots brief? Ladies and gentlemen, after eight years of training countless people, I can say this: It's not the way you do it in business. A fighter pilot's briefing isn't an informal get-together where ideas are exchanged. That's already been done. There was plenty of time for ideas in the Future Picture stage and plenty of time for ideas in the strategy and courses-of-action stage. Now come the details of the tactics. The fighter pilot's brief is where our men and women are told about a mission that could cost them their lives, so you'd better believe these people are paying attention to how the briefer looks, what he says, and how he says it.

When one walks into a fighter pilot's briefing room, first impressions are everything. There should be no doubt in the minds of the squadron members that the flight leader, the person responsible for that briefing, has been in that room two, three, maybe even four hours before the brief even started. Whiteboards are spaced around the room with the mission objective laid out in neatly lettered printing. The timelines and the decision matrix have ruler-straight lines; the tactics are arranged in colors to indicate different areas of responsibilities; even the chairs are spaced perfectly in front of the table. When the flight leader has it done right, the pilots are ready to give him or her instantaneous buy-in. They're willing to follow this person into downtown Baghdad, in the most heavily defended area in Iraq, because when they walk into that briefing room they can see *immediately* that they've got a no-kidding, buttoned-up flight leader taking them there.

Are your briefings like that in the business world? Do your meetings start on time, when you say they will? Has the projector been set up ahead of time? Is all data loaded? Is there a spare CD? Are you using a computer? Did you check the interface to the projector? Is there a back-up plan in case the computer fails? Are there whiteboards and other visuals to help the learning experience and are they absolutely free of spelling errors? *Does the totality of the room tell your team that you're prepared and ready to go?*

One of the most successful advertising agencies is located in, of all places, Oklahoma City. This is a Leaning-Forward fighter pilot–style organization. Advertising has a creative flair, so the agency's briefing rooms, their new business rooms, are designed for theatrical impact. The walls are black; the seats are in a semicircle facing two plasma monitors that drop down from the ceiling. There are high-speed broadband connections that connect in real time to recording studios in Hollywood and film production companies in New York. The lights are recessed; the audio system is state-of-the-art digital. When the agency presents advertising, they present it with flair. But even before the presentation begins, you'd already bought in when you walked into that room.

That's the way it is in the fighter pilot world because the briefing is everything, communication is critical, confidence in the plan is a must, and preparation is key.

Not surprisingly, preparing a great brief takes time. Let's start at the beginning. The day of the mission, the flight leaders show up at the squadron two or three hours before the brief is to take place to put their materials up on the whiteboards or put their audiovisuals together. You probably do that, too. Next, almost without exception, the flight leader sits down and actually *visualizes* the mission. Fighter pilots call that chair-flying. In his head, sitting in that chair, his hands placed on the throttles and the stick, he goes through the mission just as it is on the whiteboards, to see if it works. Athletes call it visualizing their moves or knowing exactly where all the players are on the field. What a great advantage this is. If you stop and chair-fly your mission, you get to visualize the mission before you set it in stone. I can't tell you how many times I realized there was a mistake in the execution phase by just chair-flying the mission before putting the briefing on.

When the time comes for you to deliver the brief, get there early, prep the briefing room, and test the brief by chair-flying the mission. Do it yourself. Before you make an important phone call, chair-fly it. What are your scripted answers to this question or that? If it's a conference call with four or five people, chair-fly the call and visualize which person on your team is going to do or say what. In a presentation to a client, take it no less seriously than pilots do a combat mission. Chair-fly *everything*. Test your plans. Find the flaws, and when your team comes in and the questions start, your answers will be so reassuring, so sound, that the buy-in only deepens as everyone sees that this mission is well thought out and entirely achievable.

THE BRIEFING

Now, let's get into the specifics of briefing. We've already talked about the importance of setting the stage, that is, prepositioning everything, preparing the boards, making sure when that door opens, at the exact, precise moment, everything is prepared. You're making a statement that you're ready to go. Cell phones are off, eyes are forward. You've got everyone's attention.

STEP ONE: SET THE TIMING

In my world, briefings start on time and end on time. If you want to set the tone of Flawless Execution, respect your team and their busy lives by starting and ending on time—every time. In my twelve years in the military I could almost bet that if our briefing was late, rushed, or sloppy, the mission execution would be the same. The way you start the mission briefing will always dictate the outcome of your execution. Sloppy brief = sloppy execution.

When your team is seated, start right off with the time hack.

"Morning, gents. Welcome to the brief. In thirty-five seconds, time will be oh-seven-hundred."

You see, in our briefing, our flight leader makes sure that everybody is synchronized, to the exact second.

"Ten seconds."

You may call it synchronization; we call it doing a time hack.

"Five, four, three, two, one, hack; oh-seven-hundred. Everybody good?"

Why is this so critical? In the air, we've got fuel limitations, weather limitations, air cover for a certain amount of time, distance issues, abort points, and exact time-over-target windows—elements built into our plans that are extremely time sensitive. We calculate our takeoff time, our airspeed, and the time between different waypoints and lay out a mission on a timeline. We expect someone to be somewhere at an exact time. If not, we have automatic contingency plans that are triggered. If we stay on our timeline and hit our window precisely, we'll be "bombs on-target on-time," the age-old expression in military aviation. No point bombing the factory after they've moved the machines.

In business, it may not come down to seconds, but timing is absolutely critical. Just like us, you have to have everybody on the same page whether you're rolling out a new product, switching out the fall inventory, or planning a software upgrade in a department. How many times has one department gotten out of sync with another or one person on the team with the rest of the team? Maybe the research and development department was very excited about a new product and leaked some details. The sales reps hear it and they get excited and with a wink and a nod tell their customers about the next big new things—and then R&D runs into a snag. The product is not available and, poof!—all the air goes out of your cycles. Far from that drumbeat of excitement, the customers are now casting a wary eye your way; there's a cold pail of water waiting for you behind the door.

Setting everyone's timing is one of the most important things that we do, right off the bat, and you need to do it, too.

STEP TWO: THE MISSION OBJECTIVE

The next thing out of the flight leader's mouth is that all-important mission objective. Think about it. Everybody is assembled in the room. The pilots have their line-up cards or notes. They're seated, eyes forward, ready to go. After the time hack, the next few minutes are critical to setting the tone for today's entire mission.

"Today's mission objective is destroy the bridge, located at north thirty-twenty-fifteen, west fifteen-forty-five-ten, by thirteen-hundred Local."

Now the flight leader has their attention. One phrase, one sentence that's clear, measurable, achievable—that is, believable—and that supports the overall Future Picture. A bombing mission and a bridge. *Today's mission objective is to destroy the bridge located at north 31-20-15, west 15-45-10, by 1300L.*

Next, lay out the secondary objectives. The pilots have got the assets in the air; they're armed and hot. What else can we do—within the parameters of the commander's intent—to further or accelerate the accomplishment of the overall Future Picture?

"With the destruction of the bridge, we're also going to destroy the machine gun nest in the target area and help out our soldiers. Finally, we're going to do all this with no losses to our forces."

In business, once you and your team pack for a trip, fly cross country, check into a hotel, and prepare for your meeting, why not try to attack some secondary objectives? Why not drive past the competitor's new plant or walk through some of those regional chains that have no outlets back east or plan a meeting with a few small accounts? For us, let's do as much damage as we can behind enemy lines. And, more importantly, let's make sure that we come away with zero losses or zero fallout. Primary and secondary objectives are critical.

STEP THREE: THE SCENARIO

Once you lay down your mission objective and your secondary objectives, let's get more buy-in. Let's brief the scenario. The scenario deepens buy-in by adding that utterly important feeling of personal empowerment. It tells us why this mission is important, why what we're about to do matters; it gives the team a sense of the stakes involved.

"Okay, today's scenario is this: A battlefield area interdiction is expected fifteen nautical miles north of the target with enemy troops. Enemy armored cavalry is going to be advancing through the forward line of troops, toward the position of the bridge. Contact with the enemy is expected in five hours. The bridge is key to their advance. If we can take out that bridge, our forces can bottle the enemy and will execute an end-around sweep to counter the attack."

What's your scenario? In 2002, AOL Time Warner was under the gun to buttress up their flagging AOL unit. They needed something dramatic, something that would keep subscribers and fight off the competitive inroads from other Internet Service Providers (ISPs). A new Future Picture was articulated, strategies were set into motion, and the programmers and developers were briefed. No doubt the hours would be long and the stress high, but they knew the scenario. MSN. While some of their problems were internal, they had one big external threat: MSN, from Microsoft. Who had more cash, more programmers, and more computer savvy than the Redmond, Washington, behemoth? Who could crush AOL? MSN was certainly the enemy, but AOL had two things going for it that MSN didn't—a huge base of customers and a rich treasure of content. AOL gave its programmers a mission: Build the latest version of America Online software with content so unique, so useful, and so exclusive that no one need seriously consider MSN. Blow them out of the water and do it fast. Little wonder that AOL Version 8.0 was on time and released to rave reviews. The team had a clear mission objective and they knew the scenario. Giving MSN an opening was a crack no one wanted to see in the dike.

Knowing the scenario makes for a team determined to achieve their objectives. They know what the stakes are, and the buy-in yet again deepens.

STEP FOUR: WEATHER AND ENVIRONMENT

Let's now look at the weather and the environment. You might be asking yourself, as a businessperson, "Weather and environment, Murph? How does that play into my briefing? How does that play into the way I'm going to go out and carry out my mission?" Stay with me.

For fighter pilots, a constant problem is the weather. It changes daily. It affects them. It affects their ability to execute. There are things pilots simply cannot do if the weather is wrong. As an absurd example, pilots obviously can't fly in a tornado, nor could they last in a bad hailstorm.

Yes, weather is literally a very significant factor in the fighter pilot business, so they brief it: "Local weather, right now, ten thousand scattered, twenty-five thousand scattered; should not be a problem for in and out of the base. For the weather around the target area, right now, it's clear with ten nautical miles visibility.

Sun angle at the time-on-target will be about seventy-five degrees up, so the shadowing effect on the terrain and the target itself should be minimal."

What's the external factor that you can't do much about, but remains critical to your mission, indeed your survival? Well, for some businesses it may literally be the weather. Only a foolish farmer would plant seeds knowing that a devastating downpour was forecast, and a lawn service wouldn't schedule to cut lawns on a rainy day. If you own a restaurant, are you briefing the weather that day or just keeping your head in the ground and setting up the outdoor patio anyway? Are you getting it?

But don't take me too literally. It's not *just* about the weather. It's about those constant, recurring factors that you have to think about every day and adjust accordingly. Are you going to quote an interest rate on a loan without looking at the prime rate?

Mortgage brokers look at mortgage rates every day.

Television stations and television networks look at their overnight ratings and juggle their schedules to improve their viewership.

Mail-order companies and TV direct-response advertisers look at their response rates daily and adjust their mailing lists or their offers or their timing.

Stockbrokers check the Dow Jones Industrial Average before every phone call and adjust their pitch.

Even newspaper publishers look at the next day's headlines hungry for the big one that will drive newsstand sales. Depending on what they see, they'll either increase or decrease the press run.

Are you starting to see the parallel? Mortgage rates are to a mortgage banker what the daily weather is to a fighter pilot. Same for stock indexes to a broker or ratings to a TV network.

That's the business version of weather—daily, recurring external factors that you need to know about before you execute your mission. It may be storming outside; it may be a stormy day on the Dow—but you better know and you need to include that in your brief.

Which brings us to environment. What is the environment? Forget the word as you know it. Environments are those large, *usually unique*, external factors that might affect our mission. For pilots, these are things like the *geography* and the *terrain* in and around the target area.

Here's what environment sounds like in the brief:

"There is a very large cliff to the west of the bridge itself, but as far as the shadowing effect it should not have much of an effect on the target. Around the target area itself, the ground is good for terrain masking, and with the clear weather we can get down low and hide in the weeds if need be."

Your environment might be social, political, or even attitudinal.

Do you need to consider the economic outlook in a specific region of the country?

Before you invest in a new technology, is that technology at risk due to a pending regulatory change?

Has the consumer sentiment changed and made your product environmentally unattractive to certain buyers—perhaps certain buyers in certain parts of the country?

Are you complying with the newest product labeling laws, or the current disclosure laws, or the recycling laws, both locally and nationally?

I guarantee you that the signage laws in Vail or Aspen, Colorado, are much different from the signage laws in New York City or Las Vegas, Nevada. You have to adjust your store design, for instance; they don't allow neon signs in Aspen.

That's environment.

Briefing: Steps Five through Seven

To err is human, to err without briefing the plan
is suicide.

After briefing the environment, the flight leader wants the pilots to physically, visually, and mentally fly against the threat even as they sit in the briefing room. He wants them to feel tension. He wants them to start sharpening their senses. He wants their mental and situational awareness radars sweeping a little faster.

STEP FIVE: THREATS AND INTELLIGENCE

The next part of the squadron's briefing covers threats to its success. In the planning phase the officers looked at all the threats standing in their way; now the flight leader must communicate to the team the significant stumbling blocks to the mission and the resources that will be applied to overcome them. Today's threats are SAM sites and enemy air-to-air assets like the Mig-29. When flight leaders brief threats, they don't just list them and tick them off like a shopping list; they dramatize them. The flight leader will show a picture of the threat, describe its performance envelope, and tell his pilots exactly how high and far their guns can shoot, what kind of warning they will have inside their cockpits when that particular threat locks on to them, and what kind of evasive maneuvers or counter tactics they can take against that threat. He's honest. He tells them these threats can kill them in the blink of an eye.

That's how the Air Force briefs a threat. Flight leaders tell the pilots what it is, what characteristics it has, and how they can avoid or defeat it.

The same thing goes in business. Look at today's threats. You have disruptive technologies like Wi-Fi, which make expensive technologies like DSL moot. How are you going to react if it gains traction? Better features, discounting—or just buy the companies deploying it?

You have financial threats. What if a key supplier goes under or your leasing company doesn't like the interest-rate landscape and closes the spigot?

You have competitive threats like a low-price electric tooth-brush called SpinBrush. What are you going to do to cope? Shift the game, match the price, or cede the category and redeploy your assets in more lucrative markets?

I assure you, when squadrons brief the threats and lay out their contingencies, a fast withdrawal is *always* one of their survival plans. No reason to be embarrassed. Dying is a lousy price to pay for misplaced pride.

Look at your threats. You have social, political, environmental, and regulatory threats; probably dozens more I couldn't even begin to imagine. They are there; you know them better than I. They affect you every day. They are a part of your industry and your environment, and now is the time to identify them and explain your counter tactics.

STEP SIX: MOTHERHOOD

The next portion of the briefing lays down the foundation for the entire mission. We call this "motherhood" or the "admin" or the "administrative standards." You know motherhood. What did your mother used to say to you before you went off to school? "Did you remember your lunchbox?" "Make sure you say 'Yes, Ma'am,' 'No, Ma'am.'" "Don't forget your homework."

Motherhood involves those things in a fighter squadron that are done on every single mission. They are *standards*. They are largely unchanging. Pilots will always taxi together as a formation, utilizing two ship lengths' spacing between their jets. They will fly to and from their training airspace at 350 knots. In the briefing, standards can be altered if the environment or a new flight leader decides to do it differently. This is why time is spent on this area. If the flight leader does not want to alter or change our standards, he or she will simply state that starts, taxis, and takeoffs today will all be performed "standard" or that *"standard motherhood is in effect today for the entire mission."*

You have standards. You have operating procedures for inputting new customers into your systems. You have standards in your credit department, standards for billing, standards for shipping, and so on. These are your standard operating procedures (SOPs), and they apply on every mission *unless you brief otherwise.*

Customer support has motherhood.

Sales has motherhood. (Most companies require a salesperson to have a standard battle kit—a sales kit, a defined set of sales literature, order forms, brochures, and so on—always packed in his or her briefcase.)

These standards are motherhood, and we tell our people that they apply to the current mission. "As we launch this product, motherhood applies across the board," would be a good statement. It means that standard credit policies are in effect, that the standard minimum ordering quantities are in effect, that the standard commissions are in effect, and so on.

If they are not, now is the time to say so. If commissions have a special override, here's where you tell the sales force. If the ordering minimums have been lowered or increased, say it here. If not, motherhood is in effect.

This part of the briefing should be very short and concise and right on target because you expect your fighter pilots to know them; they're standardized procedures.

STEP SEVEN: TACTICS AND TIMELINE

After motherhood we get into the meat of the mission. Let's think about what we've covered so far. We've laid down our timing. We know what our primary mission objective is and also our secondary objectives. We know about weather and the environment. We know about the motherhood or the administrative standards. We also know about threats. And now it's time to go out and turn and burn. This is where you, as a flight leader, will shine. This is where science, art, individuality, and your studies all come together. Now it's time for tactics.

Tactics is where flight leaders go over step five in detail, the course(s) of action, and the timeline associated with them. This is where 75 percent of the briefing time is spent. This is where the real stuff is discussed. This is not where pilots talk about how they're going to take off or how they're going to land or how they're going to refuel. Now is the time to talk about *exactly* how they're going to carry out the mission. They're going to talk about *when* they're going to commit, *how* they're going to do it, *what* their formations are going to look like, and *what* weapons they're going to select. They're also going to talk about their decisions—whether they're going to continue with the attack or fall back or go neutral or abort because the forces are just too big or the odds are just not in their favor.

What's the objective here? To make it simple. To lay out all the possible scenarios and the scripted responses and make the briefing understandable. Flight leaders don't want fighter pilots to have to think very hard when they're engaged in combat. So one thing they do is to brief in detail the *decision matrix*. As a review from the planning chapter, let me give you an example. Pilots are en route to the target, a SAM site. At five minutes out from the target, they'll arm up the jets and *precommit*. At two minutes out, the flight leader will make the "commit" call and they'll head in.

All of this is briefed using a decision matrix. Decisions are laid out on a timeline and they brief what we're going to do in specific increments. Five minutes out. Two minutes out. Here's what to do if things look good. Here's what to do if we have an abort, a change in weather, anything that may change the decision to proceed. All of this is scripted before takeoff and laid into a decision matrix, which is woven into the timeline and briefed to all the pilots.

As I said earlier, timing is everything to a fighter pilot. Little wonder that a timeline is the key on the decision matrix. Every event on the decision matrix has a time hack. The first major threat is expected sixty seconds before the target area. At thirty seconds before bomb release, we'll be in the range of triple A and some small arms fire. At thirty seconds after impact, the SAM threats will be sanitized. At ninety seconds, the last jet should be pulling off target, and the window closes. The squadron is pushing out of the area. At each of these time hacks pilots have three, maybe four decisions to make—each with scripted, actionable responses. If it looks bad at sixty seconds, they will either abort, press on, or engage the enemy in air-to-air combat.

The point is, pilots don't know what will happen, but they do know what they'll do when it does. Your tactics and timing should be the same. Every business works on a timeline. Give your team their timeline, make it clear, and factor in variances within the scope of a decision matrix so they'll have agreed-upon responses scripted before they go execute.

Briefing: Steps Eight and Nine

STEP EIGHT: CONTINGENCIES

The planning done for contingencies is a critical part of a fighter pilot's briefing. Briefings are always wrapped up with the contingencies. Pilots ask themselves the very, very difficult question, "What if?" What if the weather changes over the target area after they launch and get airborne? What if the air refueling tanker does not show up and they can't take on fuel? What if the flight leader blows up in midair before they get over the target area?

Now pilots don't want to be overwhelmed with all the contingencies. They talk about the contingencies based on that mission; current intelligence, current tactics, current weather, and environmental conditions. What if a competitor gets wind of your plans and decides to flood your market with discounts for their products? Will you delay your plans or increase your discounts— or what?

What if you have a grand opening and more people than you ever thought possible show up? Do you have a backup plan to rush inventory to the store? (I can't tell you how often a store will run a door-buster sale only to run out of stock. You can get away with that once, but if it happens twice, you'll lose consumer trust.)

Contingencies cover the entire mission. You identify "what-ifs," beginning at the first hour of your mission and going all the way to the very end.

I'll give you an example of a Leaning-Forward fighter pilot–type team that briefs contingencies as well as anyone in the nation: Monday Night Football. This is a live event that is as full of potential problems as any "mission" in the world. In the comfort of your home, the broadcast is smooth and even, but how did that come about? The Monday Night Football team briefs and debriefs as well as any fighter squadron in the world. They plan for the weather, they analyze power grids (external factors!), they even have scripts for their broadcasters that smooth over the uneven quality of the teams playing so that no matter what, football fans will be interested in watching (a serious factor toward the end of the season).

Then there are the uncountable variables during a game. Players are moving across a 100-yard-long football field with over a dozen cameras trained on them. There are literally miles of cables and wireless devices linking those cameras to a broadcast truck where the director "mixes" the myriad shots into a finished product that is then fed live to the satellite. That satellite then broadcasts the signal to hundreds of television stations and cable systems, which in turn deliver the broadcast to your home.

Despite all of the variables and potential traps, rare is the day that a key play isn't captured on at least three cameras. Rarer still is a moment of dead air time. These broadcast crews work with military precision. They have backups for backups and scripted responses for every possible failure in the entire chain between the football field and your home television set.

And they debrief after every broadcast so they do it better next week.

You brief contingencies now so your men and women aren't brainstorming when it's too late—during the execution phase. In the heat of battle, time is everything; you want to be quick. You want to react to situations based on decisions that have already been made—*scripted responses*—and that's what the contingency phase accomplishes. Let's make those decisions now, in the comfort of our briefing room, so two hours later, when we're in the heat of the battle, when we're turning and burning, we have responses to almost any contingency.

STEP NINE: WRAP UP

Now, let's wrap up the briefing. We want to make sure that nobody has a question, that there's no confusion. Because missions have so many interconnected parts, we like to go through the entire brief and hold questions to the end. Make sure that nobody walks out of that room with a question in their mind on how they're going to execute the mission. That's the accountability loop that will start our after-mission debrief. No questions? Good. Now let's leave the room on a high note. Leaders need to motivate their troops to march on Troy. You've been deepening their buy-in at each step of the brief. Now give them a "God Bless America." It's not corny. It's true. And they want to hear it.

CHAPTER 12 ▶▶▶▶▶▶▶▶▶▶▶ ✈ ▶▶▶▶▶▶▶

Execute

Task saturation is the silent killer to execution.

Now it's time to strap the jets on and go turn and burn—it's time to execute. How do fighter pilots execute complex missions? So far they've taken the Future Picture and determined strategies or centers of gravity their tactical teams will target. Through the prism of the six steps they have developed a tactical plan. Then they briefed that plan. How, then, do they execute?

Fighter pilots hate surprises. I've said that before but I'll say it again. Between the time they close the door behind them and head out to the jets, and the time they return from their mission, *they want the mission to be the brief.* They want the mission to be so precise that they're simply acting out the script, walking through their lines, hitting their cues just like an actor in a well-rehearsed play. If the plan calls for their jets to be lined up on the runway at 0600, then they expect to be lined up at 0600. The head nods go up and down the line at exactly the time hack specified, they tank with the refuelers exactly when they planned to tank, the jets roll in and come off target on time, and they land almost to the minute.

When pilots execute a mission, the brief *is* the mission. They're one and the same. In fact, so literally do they fly their brief that few pilots know what to say after a mission other than to say, "It went as planned." If you watched the news during Desert Storm, what seemed like a lot of camera-shy pilots with microphones thrust in their faces was in fact this very truth playing out on a real stage. Pilots simply don't know what to say—even to an inquiring reporter—other than to say, "It went as planned."

Why is this? I knew a young pilot who was graduating from training at the Navy's flight school at Pensacola. His father was there, and he asked his son what was so different about flight school. The son said: "Studying at college was a hit-or-miss affair. Here, our lives depend on everything we do." In the execution phase of a mission, pilots' lives depend on the brief, and they want things to be as close to the brief as humanly possible. They want the mission to feel like the unfolding of a Broadway play. No glitches. No missed lines. No extra scenes. Timing that works, jokes that work, singers that sing when the orchestra starts to play. They want it to "go as planned," which to the fighter pilot means it went "as briefed."

Not that things don't get in the way. They do. The biggest stumbling block to Flawless Execution, no matter how great your plan or how detailed your briefing, is something we call the silent killer—*task saturation*. Task saturation is too much to do with not enough time, not enough tools, and not enough resources to get the mission accomplished. It can be real or imagined, but in the end it can do the same thing. It can kill you.

I had two friends who both flew perfectly good jets into the ground. Were they good pilots? You bet. What happened? They succumbed to task saturation. I bet if you had tapped them on the shoulder five seconds before ground impact and asked them how things were going in the cockpit, they would have given you a thumbs up and said things were great—it was a piece of cake—

and then, boom, they hit the ground. They were so focused on a climbing workload that they lost track of the ground. They died task saturated. And they never knew it.

Unfortunately, most people, or companies for that matter, wear task saturation like a badge of honor. "I've been on the road for five days, made nine presentations, wrote up specifications for a new bid in the hotel room, missed lunch, went into the office Saturday, got caught up on my paperwork, and now I'm heading to New York," said one salesman as he boarded his flight, the stress etched across his face. Or a software programmer: "We've been in the office for three days straight, some of us sleeping on the floor, another guy walking around like a zombie with his hand tied to a coffee pot. We have two million lines of code to untangle."

The surprising thing is that most people are proud that they're overworked. Perhaps it makes them feel wanted or it makes them feel valuable; they feel that they are a key employee, but in truth it's not good for the company. What fighter pilots know about task saturation should worry every CEO. As task saturation increases, performance decreases; as task saturation increases, executional errors increase. Task saturation is a silent killer, and in these days of layoffs and asking people to do more with less, task saturation is truly a killer in corporate America. Rather than wear it like a badge of honor, businesses need to deal with it and deal with it now. The correct action to take is to acknowledge that it exists, acknowledge that it creates problems, identify the symptoms, and then work to eliminate it.

Thankfully, there are ways to do just that. The symptoms of task saturation have been studied and are well known. At some point in flight school I was asked to go into a room and write down three things that happen to me when I become task saturated. I had never stopped to think about it until then, but I collected my thoughts and wrote down three things. The following

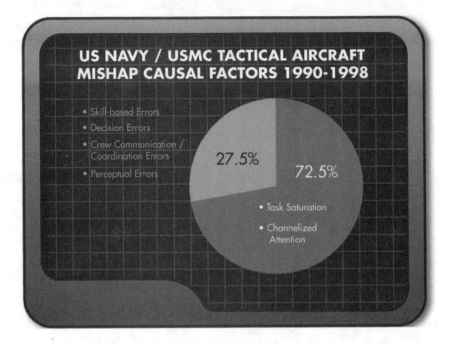

month, I was asked to do it again and again I wrote down the same three things. I had to do it a third time and, guess what—I wrote down the same three things again.

Each of us responds differently to task saturation but measured over time our individual coping mechanisms tend to be the same. We either quit, compartmentalize, or channelize. In any of these "states," you're performance is degrading and trouble is brewing.

Let's look at these three symptoms in detail.

The first coping mechanism is to shut down. You quit. You stop performing. Some people literally go blank. You open your briefcase and look at all the things that need to be done. It's just too much, so you close the briefcase, fold your hands on top, and stare at the ceiling. Same at your desk. You look at all the papers; it's too much, so you spin your chair and start staring out the window. Have you ever just said, "It's time to go take a gym break or go outside and talk to my coworkers," or "I've just had enough.

I'm leaving for the day"? That's a very obvious way of dealing with task saturation and, in moderation, it's fine. In the extreme, it brings a company to its knees.

Quitters don't say much, don't do much, and often leave the office. "Happy" quitters are always at the water cooler, in the bathroom checking their tie, or stopping by your office for a rather pointless chat.

Shutting down is the most harmless of the coping mechanisms. When you leave your desk or amble around the office, people at least know you're not executing your mission, you're not on task. You may get a bad reputation for "leaving early" or not pulling your weight, but at least you're not masking your mental "collapse."

Compartmentalizers and channelizers, on the other hand, are risky people because they *act* busy but do little, and kill you while they're at it. Have you ever let yourself get compartmentalized? Have you ever wanted to put everything in a nice, neat, linear format and arrange things just so, when all the while things are really backing up and pressures outside your compartmentalized little world are rising? Compartmentalizers start making lists, organizing their projects, and shuffling things around as if the list making and the shuffling are akin to doing the work, which they are not. Then they start going top to bottom, ticking off one item after another. They become obsessively linear, first-things-first, one project at a time.

The compartmentalizer operates in a mode that is extremely dangerous to the company. Think about the swirl of activity in a hospital emergency room. Patients are arriving, others are waiting; some patients are getting restless and irritable, and others are stalking the nurses' station. There are announcements on the PA and doctors moving from one bed to another.

If someone starts to become overloaded, the system is jeopardized. If someone reaches task saturation and compartmentalizes, the environment starts to get dangerous. Why? Because compartmentalizers *look* busy. They are hard to ferret out. You can't tell they're not getting anything done, and that hurts the system. No one knows a problem is building. No one knows a weak link has entered the chain.

Then there are those who channelize. Eighty percent of people that succumb to task saturation cope with it by channelizing, or becoming intensely focused on just one thing. Some people call this *target fixation*. "Can't you see I'm busy!" is a common answer when you interrupt a channelizer. I know you've been there before. Most of us arrive at the office with more to do than we can possibly get done in a day—and then unplanned events kick in and start to task saturate us. You get a call: "Honey, the kid is sick at school. Can you pick him up?" Then your biggest client calls: "You need to deliver a document to me by one o'clock today." Ever been there before? Of course you have; we all have. You're task saturated; you're sweating this overload of multiple priorities and you start to channelize. What's the most important thing to accomplish? Get that report out by one o'clock. What do you do? Cell phone; turn it off. Desk telephone; off the hook. Slam the door and tell everybody "No calls!" and dig into the one o'clock deadline.

You dig and dig and dig and put everything into that report, but guess what? No one picked up your sick child.

Another client called with an urgent question and you missed it.

A simple problem flares up into a major problem.

The error chain begins.

Channelizers are easy to spot. They shun eye contact when they take a bathroom break. They wave people off with a flip of the wrist. Their body language says: "Don't ask." But channelizers are almost as dangerous as compartmentalizers. In the military, our safety officer has videotape of a heart-wrenching example of channelized attention. A flight of four ground-attack fighters are working over a target at a bombing range. One after the other they come in, the jets jinking down toward the target for a low-level strafing run. Then comes the third of the four pilots. He descends, comes around the foothills, drops into the valley, pops up in altitude to visually acquire the target, rolls over to line up the target, and starts a rapid descent into his dive-bomb pass, the altimeter spinning down closer and closer to the ground. The pilot squeezes the trigger, his guns fire, and *boom* . . . the jet crashes into the ground.

Here's the chain of events: Task saturation triggered channelized attention. The pilot fixated on the target and he flew into the ground. He shut out everything except the target. He forgot to fly his jet. His coping mechanism cost him his life.

We think channelized attention is such a deadly *but preventable* obstacle to Flawless Execution that we take great pains to illustrate just how insidious it is. To do that, we tell the story of Flight 401.

On December 29, 1972, Eastern Airlines flight 401 was inbound to Miami International airport. The normal cockpit crew of three pilots was flying the plane. It was wintertime, a crystal clear night; weather was not a factor. As the first officer rolls the L-1011 out on a ten-mile final approach into Miami International he looks to the left and says to the captain: "Captain, let's put the landing gear down."

The captain looks at the copilot and says, "Roger"; he reaches up and grabs the gear handle and puts it in the down position. They look for three lights to illuminate on the forward instrument panel, indicating that the right main, the left main, and the nose wheel gear are down and locked and in a safe position to land.

However, on this ill-fated night, only two out of the three green lights illuminate: the right main, the left main, but not the nose wheel light. So the captain says, "We have an emergency procedure checklist for this. Let's get it out and read it." The emergency checklist directs the crew to raise the handle up and down to recycle the gear, but, again, they only get two green lights.

Here's the actual audio transcript pulled off the flight data recorder:

MIAMI APPROACH:	"Eastern 401, heavy. Continue approach to 9-left."
FLIGHT 401:	"Continue approach, Roger."
COCKPIT, CAPT.:	"I'm going to try down [lower the gear handle] one more time."
COCKPIT, COPILOT:	"You want me to test the lights or not?"
COCKPIT, CAPT.:	"Yeah, check it."
COCKPIT, COPILOT:	"Watch [inaudible]."
COCKPIT, COPILOT:	"Doug, it could be the light. Could you jiggle the light? It's got to come out a little and then snap in."
COCKPIT, COPILOT:	"I'll put 'em on. Up to 2,000? You want me to fly, Doug?"
COCKPIT, CAPT.:	"Yeah. What frequency is approach on?"
COCKPIT, COPILOT:	"Twenty-eight-six."
COCKPIT, CAPT.:	"I'll talk to him."
COCKPIT, CAPT.:	"Alright. Approach control, Eastern 401, we're right over the airport, here, and climbing to 2,000 feet. In fact, we've just reached 2,000 feet, and we've got to get a green light on our nose gear."
MIAMI APPROACH:	"Eastern 401. Roger. Turn left, heading 3-6-0. Maintain 2,000 [inaudible] left final."
COCKPIT, CAPT.:	"Left to 3-6-0."

COCKPIT, CAPT.:	"I think it's about the red one."
COCKPIT, COPILOT:	"Yeah, I can't get it from here. I can't make it pull out, either. We got pressure?"
COCKPIT, FLIGHT ENGINEER:	"Yes, sir, all systems."
COCKPIT, CAPT:	"Put the damn thing on autopilot."
COCKPIT, COPILOT:	"Alright."
COCKPIT, CAPT.:	[To copilot] "See if you can put that light out. Well, you've got to push the switch just a little bit further forward. Now, turn it to the right a little bit. No, I don't think it's going to fit. Hey [to the flight engineer], get down there and see if that damn nose wheel's down."
COCKPIT, COPILOT:	"Okay. You got a handkerchief or something, so I can get a little better grip on this? Anything I can do it with? This damn thing just won't come out, Doug. If I had a pair of pliers, I could get to it—"
COCKPIT, CAPT.:	"To hell with it. To hell with this. Go down and see if that red line is lined up down there. Don't screw around with that twenty-cent piece of light equipment.
COCKPIT, CAPT. TO MIAMI APPROACH:	"Eastern 401. I'll go out west, just a little further, if we can, here, and see if we can get this light to come on."
MIAMI APPROACH:	"Alright."
COCKPIT, COPILOT:	"It's always something. We could have made schedule."

COCKPIT, CAPT.:	"We can tell if the damn gear is down by looking down at the indicators.
COCKPIT, COPILOT:	It's got to be a faulty light. Doug, this damn thing just won't come out."
COCKPIT, CAPT.:	"Alright. Just leave it there."
MIAMI APPROACH:	"Eastern 401, how are things coming along out there?"
COCKPIT:	"1-8-0. . . ."

Well, at this point, our first officer, our flying pilot, decides to come up for air and starts flying again. Have you noticed that no one was talking about actually flying this large, complex jumbo jet? Three pilots, and they are all leaning forward, bent down to work on a light bulb. Well, the plane was in trouble but no one knew it. Someone bumped the control yoke (wheel) and disengaged the autopilot and the jet had been in a slow descent. Not that they knew it. They had a light bulb to worry about. The sky was ink black. The water and everglades below were also black. No reference to a horizon. So what does this pilot see? One hundred feet on the altimeter. What does he expect to see? Two thousand feet. He has twelve-seconds to react—*always trust your instruments*—but he's so task saturated (along with his two other crew members) that his pilot instincts are long gone and in twelve seconds he, and ninety-nine people aboard that night, die.

COCKPIT, COPILOT:	"Hey, we lost some of the altitude here."
COCKPIT, CAPT.:	"What?"
COCKPIT, COPILOT:	"We're still at 2,000, right?"
COCKPIT, CAPT.:	"Hey, what's happening here?"

And then the plane slams into the Everglades.

Coping Mechanisms and Task Shedding

Never, never leave your wingman.

Everyone reacts differently to task saturation. One CEO admitted to me that when he gets overloaded he stops checking the messages on his cell phone. Sounds innocent enough except when one message is about an acquisition, another that your car is in the shop, and the third that the union just went out on strike. Not a good way to handle task saturation.

I know another person who is a compulsive list maker. Have you ever seen a nurse in a hospital throw up her hands and say, "I need to organize these charts!"? Instead of doing anything, one CEO starts writing lists. A list for this and a list for that. He's task saturated. He's shutting down and doing nothing but doodling!

So what do you do about task saturation? First, hold meetings and explain the coping mechanisms. Tell people about task saturation and the common symptoms—shutting down, compartmentalizing, and channelizing. Describe these symptoms fully and use illustrations from this chapter or from your own life to make the picture as vivid as possible. Then have everyone list the three things they do to cope. More often than not, properly trained people will then recognize task saturation when it starts to hit them and they will adjust as they see themselves reverting to an inappropriate coping mechanism.

Next, try to eliminate task saturation in your workplace. Kill the weeds before they choke the grass. This doesn't mean lighten the workload but, rather, build into your company standards three simple processes that fighter pilots use to keep task saturation at bay: checklists, cross-checks, and mutual support. They're easy, so I'll go through them quickly.

CHECKLISTS

The first tool fighter pilots have to eliminate task saturation is their checklist. As a matter of fact, a checklist is so important to us that we would never dream of flying without one.

I'm sure you're familiar with checklists, but let me tell you how pilots configure theirs. For them, a checklist is a condensed portion of the flight manual—the standard operating procedures. It's a memory jogger. It's based on training, people's experience, and the standard operating procedures of our company. It's designed to get pilots pointed in the right direction very quickly by taking an action that pulls them through task saturation.

There are two types of checklists: a normal procedures section and the black-striped pages, or the emergency procedures section.

The normal procedures checklist is pretty straightforward. It's how to do everyday things—how to start the engine, how to configure the aircraft for takeoff, the air-refueling checklist, the landing. Gear down. Flaps down twenty degrees. Three-and-a-half degrees on the glideslope. Basic reminders, but good ones. On every mission, they literally open the checklists, balance it on their kneeboards, and, like little children, go through each item as if they've never landed before. It sounds incredibly unnecessary but it drops the stress levels instantly, and that helps hold task saturation at bay. Landing checklist; landing gear. Flaps. Hydraulic pressure. Fuel state. Weapons secured. Winds. Final approach traffic? Runway clear? No matter how many times they've landed, they go through the pre-landing checklists because it takes away a big hunk of the workload and saves them the stress of forgetting something critical. (To this day, highly experienced pilots still forget to drop the landing gear!)

Everyday procedures are difficult to take seriously—you think you know them and to have a checklist seems absolutely juvenile—but because they're repetitive, they tend to numb you. Why allow task saturation to creep into the system when you have an out? If fighter pilots can humble themselves and go through a checklist on how to land an airplane, can't you? In business a normal-procedures checklist would be things like how to open the store, how to stock the store, how to close the store; everything, step by step, based on your standard operating procedures. The Batesville Casket Company relies on checklists in their everyday operation. From pre-funeral arrangements to meeting with the grieving family, Batesville has a check list that helps its customers maneuver through this difficult event by using time tested methodologies of a successful funeral experience.

In other cases, common business etiquette, like a meeting agenda, masks the powerful tool of a checklist hidden within. A well-organized PowerPoint presentation hides a lifesaving check-list parading as bullet points and talk points. People often scoff at our insistence on checklists, but they can get you through the flurry of activity that inevitably precedes a meeting (did you remember to configure a back-up computer for the biggest presentation of your career?) with something to jog your memory, lower the *need* to remember, and lower the stress.

Training is an area where checklists are an absolute. Do you incorporate a checklist in the training of a new hire? When you're training a new store associate, do you have them walk

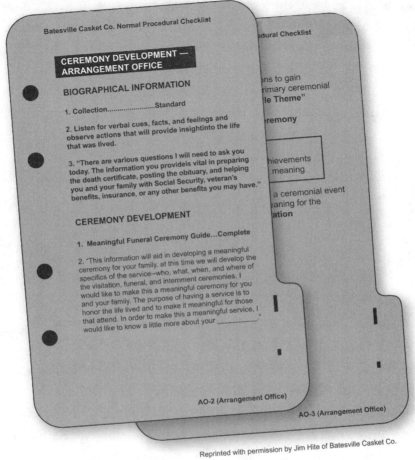

CEREMONY DEVELOPMENT —
ARRANGEMENT OFFICE

BIOGRAPHICAL INFORMATION

1. Collection.......................Standard

2. Listen for verbal cues, facts, and feelings and observe actions that will provide insight into the life that was lived.

3. "There are various questions I will need to ask you today. The information you provide is vital in preparing the death certificate, posting the obituary, and helping you and your family with Social Security, veteran's benefits, insurance, or any other benefits you may have."

CEREMONY DEVELOPMENT

1. Meaningful Funeral Ceremony Guide...Complete

2. "This information will aid in developing a meaningful ceremony for your family. at this time we will develop the specifics of the service–who, what, when, and where of the visitation, funeral, and internment ceremonies. I would like to make this a meaningful ceremony for you and your family. The purpose of having a service is to honor the life lived and to make it meaningful for those that attend. In order to make this a meaningful service, I would like to know a little more about your _____."

AO-2 (Arrangement Office)

AO-3 (Arrangement Office)

Reprinted with permission by Jim Hite of Batesville Casket Co.

along with your favorite manager in the hope that they'll pick up good habits? But is that person really learning the standard operating procedures of your store, or is he or she picking up the good (and possibly bad) habits of that person they're training with?

At Afterburner, we introduce checklists to new hires on their very first day, and we use them in every facet of our business. New hires start with our standards manual, and then we have them "walk the store" with an experienced team member. When they're done, they're on their own, but they have a checklist to fall back on when it gets too busy. Why leave anything to chance? Will the new hire remember every detail about conducting our seminars from his training, or reading our 260-page standards guide? Checklists reinforce this training and leave nothing to chance.

One of our clients uses a checklist to ensure that the first day of work for new hires is a positive and rewarding experience. Instead of losing the time to chaos or solitude, the new hire has a "passport" that has to be stamped as he meets critical people or is introduced to important functions. At first it seemed trivial, but, after the three days of a well-thought-out flight plan through the corporate headquarters, the new hire felt confident and part of the team. He knew how to get around, who did what and how to conduct the functions of the company. His passport was his checklist.

The black-stripe pages are known as the emergency procedures section. This is the checklist that comes into play when the problems are life threatening. These are one-liners that can be read in an instant. Pilots go right to a page that fits the problem and they see memory joggers and actions to take to solve the problem quickly.

In a simplified form, you have black-stripe pages posted next to the fire extinguishers and near complex machines—and if you dissect your business, you'll see the need for them at cash registers and other "choke points" in your operations where delays, compounded by the absence of a supervisor, can grind your operation to a halt. Find your choke points and build in a stress-reducing checklist that the everyday employee can revert to.

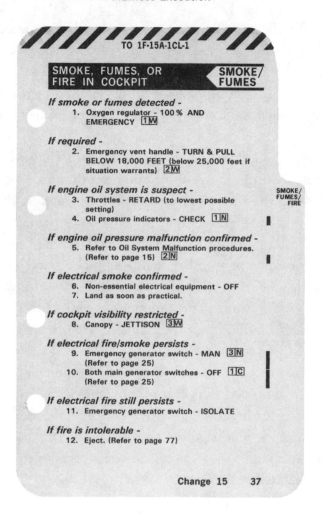

CROSS-CHECKS

The pilot's second tool is cross-checks. Imagine, if you will, what it's like for single-seat fighter pilots monitoring 350 switches and dials, all at one time. How do they assimilate all the data? How do they keep everything straight? How do they stay focused on the overall mission objective and still fly the aircraft?

That's where cross-checks come into play. Cross-checks are so important that pilots call them their "Cross-checks to Success."

Among those 350 instruments in the cockpit are four or five instruments that they *really* pay attention to. The primary aircraft control instrument is called the attitude indicator. Some of you may know of this instrument as the artificial horizon. It is basically a ball in fluid. The lower part of the ball, the brown part of the ball, represents the ground, while the blue part represents the sky. If a pilot sees more brown than blue, the aircraft is in a dive. If he or she sees more blue than brown, the aircraft is in a climb. And if the ball is tilted left or right, the aircraft is in a banked turn.

Another key instrument is the altimeter. Am I at 2,000 feet? Well, yes, I am. Back to the attitude indicator. Everything okay? Yes. Are my wings still level? I'm in a slight bank; I fix that. Then I go to another instrument. The heading indictor—am I on course? Am I heading 2-7-0 degrees? Yes, I am. Back to the attitude indicator. Okay. Then VVI—the Vertical Velocity Indicator. Am I going up or down? Up? Okay. Back to the attitude indicator. Back to the altimeter. Back to the heading. And so on.

This is the hub and spoke of a cockpit cross-check. Back and forth to the key instruments, always including a regular scan of the attitude indicator in between. Eyes moving quickly from one instrument back to the attitude indicator, never channelizing, always scanning.

How does that translate to business? For most companies, your attitude indicator is customer satisfaction. You read this every day, every hour. Are your customers happy? Do they rate your service highly? Then on to the rest of your instruments. These are determined by the priorities of your business. Maybe it's the sales funnel—how many prospects are working their way toward a sale? Or maybe it's click-through on a website or perhaps it's your seller feedback on eBay. If you own restaurants, it may be the wait time, the table turns, and beverage sales as a percentage of your total sales.

Have you defined your instrument panel, do you get data inputs from your instruments with regularity, and then, do you have a smooth, disciplined cross-check, just like fighter pilots do in the cockpit? Are you maintaining aircraft control? Are you taking care of the customer? Are you getting too focused on a new marketing plan or spending too much time on human resources while customer service is waning? You have to have an instrument panel. Every company needs one. And the data displayed on that panel needs to be updated with absolute regularity. Then it's up to you. You have to watch it and adjust, and that means you must have some form of a consistent cross-check, just like we do.

MUTUAL SUPPORT

The last tool that we use to eliminate task saturation is called mutual support. We never go anywhere—anywhere—without a wingman. We fly as a team, usually in two-ship or four-ship formations. My wingman is my partner. He's physically positioned where he can assist me if I get into trouble. He's checking my six, my blind spots, my tail. All we have to do is turn our head ninety degrees, and we can check our wingman's six or pull one another back into formation.

Do you know enough about the other person's role in the cubicle right next door, in the office across the hall, across town, or across the country, to be their wingman and check their six? Do you know enough about what's going on in other people's cockpits to help them?

Mutual support requires that we learn each other's roles and rely on each other. The more I know about your job, the better I can provide mutual support for you.

But far more importantly, you can eliminate task saturation and improve your fighting odds if you literally go into major meetings as teams. Words are the swords in the combat of business, and two people do a better job than one of "hearing" what's said and fielding questions. Operating as a team allows for latitude in negotiations and role playing in the meeting, and gives you someone who's backing you up and hearing what you miss.

Any discussion on task saturation wouldn't be complete without a comment on communication. Fighter pilots support each other by being concise. They call it *combat communication*. Combat communication involves speaking with clear, concise words, without a lot of filler material. They say what they need to say, concisely, and then get off the radio as quickly as possible. Why do they insist on this? Chatter distracts us from more important messages, and if the radios are being used for extraneous conversation, the really important messages are blocked out.

How do you communicate? Are your really important messages being blocked out by extraneous conversation—chatter? Are you really communicating in a clear, concise manner, as if lives depend on it?

Then consider data. Data is communication; in fact, data is one of the areas of communication that needs to be cleaned up first. Are you generating reams of interesting but time-consuming data? Spreadsheet software is a wonderful convenience, but it is easily abused. Most businesses we see are passing around spreadsheets that would take a week to unpack. Few people realize the extent to which they've allowed data to clutter communication and trigger task saturation.

In business, in the execution engine, have at least two people in any important meeting. You hear one thing, while your partner picks up something you missed.

Have a checklist—an agenda—to keep you on point.

If you're closing a sale, have a checklist with your contract lest you fill it out and need to go back for a re-sign. Re-signs are a good way to lose a sale.

Create your instrument panel and steer your company by it.

Time and again, customers will ask for variances. If everyone knows the instrument panel, you can rest assured that bad variances, an overly discounted contract, and the like won't creep into the system.

And take the time to talk about task saturation. You'd be surprised how much change you can engineer by simple education. This is it; this is how to overcome it—and your people are one step closer to Flawless Execution.

Debrief

It's not *who's* right, it's *what's* right.

I think fighter pilots were born to debrief. Consider their training. As fledgling pilots, they are so green they don't hope for much more than to survive to fly another day. That's why they are debriefed after every flight.

As they blossom into tactical fighter pilots, they debrief to improve their skills.

Finally as they approach the point of the spear and become combat pilots, they debrief to win.

Survive–improve–win. That is what it's all about. The same thing applies to you in the business world. When you start a company, your first debriefs allow you to survive your inexperience. As your market share expands, your debriefs help you hold on to what you've got and pass around best practices. And when a competitor throws everything at you, the debrief is already in place and you have a mechanism for rapid response. Maybe for saving your entire company.

Unfortunately, only a small percentage of companies in corporate America have any system for looking back and evaluating execution errors and successes. Debriefs don't occur at the end of a project, at the end of the week, at the end of the month, or at the end of the fiscal year. Why? Two primary reasons stand out. First, because *time is money*. In the world of billable hours, it's on to the next project, the next week, the next month, the next fiscal year, or the next client. Second, there is an understandable perception that, in business, rank and egos impede a true debrief.

Consider this: *You cannot afford to skip debriefing*. For a fighter pilot, it's life or death. Rank or ego? You think fighter pilots don't have egos. And rank? That's the name of the game in the military. The debrief is the most powerful tool that you can bring to the business world. It is where information feeds back into the company. It's where things done right—and things done wrong— are identified. It's how companies truly learn from their experiences and react, just as we fighter pilots do, almost in real time.

How does one put debrief into proper perspective? Theorists would hold that execution is the most important part of business. I don't disagree, but as we discussed earlier, the brief and the mission should be one and the same. Brief the mission, visualize it in your head, fly it. That's the way pilots do it. The execution should in some ways be largely anticlimactic. If you're doing things right—which is the goal, after all—you'll know the outcome before you execute.

That certainly doesn't mean that pilots don't have problems or that a well-trained hostile aircraft can never get the better of us. Fighter pilots get shot down, antiaircraft fire takes out our bombers, and things do go wrong. In the unfolding of a play, actors will miss their cues, musicians miss a beat, and a light might not turn on at exactly the right moment. We did well in Desert Storm—nearly as flawless an air campaign as can be—but we had losses. That's why I argue that in the fullness of the Flawless Execution Model, from the 30,000-foot perspective, the most important phase is the debrief. It is at once a squadron's critique, its training, its intelligence gathering, the transfer mechanism for lessons learned, the catalyst to accelerate the learning process and increase experience, the foundation of the next mission brief—it's all these and more. Pilots do it after a good mission, a great mission, a horrible mission, or an abort. They find out why the actor missed the cue or the light did not turn on at the exact moment, and they fix it.

First, let's get the lay of the land. Pilots fly their mission, come back to base, land, taxi to the shelters, and get out of their jets. Mission over? Not a chance. While it's all fresh in their heads, they walk straight to the briefing room and tear apart the mission. They immediately begin their debrief—a process that is utterly thorough. Their philosophy? Even the tiniest mistake could kill someone if we don't put it on the table and hash it out. Lives are on the line, and even on a good mission bad things happened. They've got to nip those things in the bud. They've got to prevent them from happening again. So they debrief. They also have to ensure that the ingredients to success are shared as well.

Let's look at the mechanics. First, in order to have an effective debrief, you bring into the room those, and only those, who were on the mission or took part in the planning of the mission. Then you must have open communication. Now, I know what you're saying. "Murph, we've *got* open communication. We go to communication seminars. We work very hard in our company on open communication." But does that mean you talk openly to a vice president above you in the company? I bet you don't. Fighter pilots learned their lessons the hard way. Covering up a problem is idiotic, so when they talk about open communication, they mean *open*—nameless, rankless debriefs. When they cross the threshold of the briefing room door, they throw away their name and rank. All they bring in is truth, an open mind, and open communication. If there was a mistake, they want to freely admit it, in front of their peers, supervisors, or subordinates; if they've forgotten a mistake, a fellow pilot is going to point it out to them. A two-star general or a green lieutenant, they're all on the same side of the table. They're one team determined not to die doing something wrong twice. Egos are absolutely gone; rank is irrelevant.

I know. You're thinking, "Must work great in the military, but I don't see it working in the civilian world. We have a rigid rank structure in our world." No question that you do. But in the fighter pilot world they have rank, too. In fact, everything done in the military hinges on rank: saluting, coming to attention, beginning sentences with the word "Sir" or "Ma'am."

But even the highest-ranking officer in the squadron is subordinate to the mission. Even the person they salute outside the debrief is objectively criticized in the debrief. Truth has to be sacred. There's simply too much at stake. Jets are volatile mixtures of fuels, bombs, and thundering, fiery afterburning engines. Surviving a flight, let alone combat, can be tough. So even the highest-ranking officer is subordinate to a truthful debrief.

Yes, it's hard to put rank aside in business. Probably for this reason and this reason alone, business has been remiss, reluctant, and perhaps shortsighted when it comes to debriefs. Thankfully, this is changing. As the message spreads and people understand the values debriefs inject into the company, companies are debriefing. What's overriding rank is a simple truth: People show their greatness in their humility, their approachability, and their ability to put the goals of the organization above their egos or rank. Winning the battles of business has priority over one's feelings. NFL officials strive for excellence, for Flawless Execution, and without a doubt are some of the best officiating crews in professional sports. Guess what one of their most important tools is? Yes. They debrief every game. Pfizer has woven full debriefs into the daily processes throughout their research and development group with great results, speeding new drugs to the market. In both cases, rank gets checked at the door.

When you put aside rank, when you get over whatever your obstacle is to debriefs, untold benefits will begin flowing into the company. Can you imagine Neil Armstrong coming back from the first moon walk and not being debriefed? If I went to visit a competitor's data center, don't you think someone from my company would want to talk to me? There is an enormous cache of valuable data, lessons learned, and a way to accelerate learning experiences ready to be discovered and passed along. This is why the Air Force holds debriefs in such high regard. This is why fighter pilots do it as a mission team, and, I can tell you for certain, why each and every pilot in a quiet moment in the day, mentally debriefs him- or herself about the smaller missions in their lives.

Once you're ready to debrief, the agenda is easy—a seven-step process. You can remember it by the acronym STEALTH.

CHAPTER 15 ▶▶▶▶▶▶▶▶▶▶▶▶▶ ✈ ▶▶▶▶

The STEALTH Debrief

Accelerating experience is the key to winning.

At Afterburner we combined our experiences as fighter pilots with our experiences as businessmen to distill the debrief process we used in fighter aviation down to a simple, seven-step business application called STEALTH. After creating STEALTH, we refined it based on our experiences using it with the hundreds of corporations we've trained. Today, STEALTH is one of the most valuable tools you can take to the office or apply to any of your missions in life.

Let's set the stage. The goal of an effective debrief is to generate valuable lessons learned, then to institutionalize those lessons learned into a core of best business practices. Once that is done, the lessons learned are transferred throughout the company. What does this accomplish? (1) Learning is accelerated, which is a process. (2) Experience is increased, which is an asset. These two combine to improve future execution, which, as we know, affects the bottom line. Imagine that a valuable lesson learned in your Miami office is transferred almost instantly to your Seattle office. Now, imagine that it's *not*. That's the power of the debrief. It identifies problems (or opportunities) and accelerates the spread of the resulting solutions.

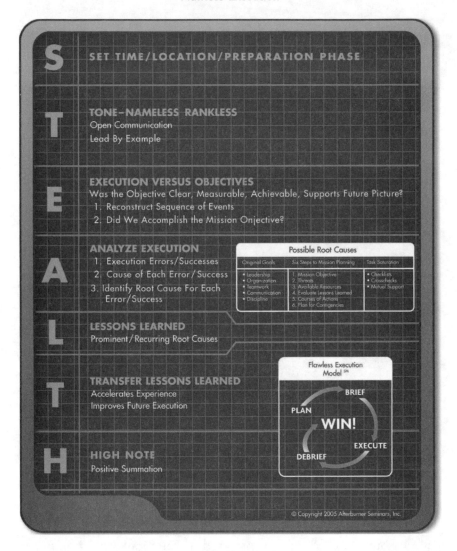

S SET TIME/LOCATION/PREPARATION PHASE

T TONE–NAMELESS RANKLESS
Open Communication
Lead By Example

E EXECUTION VERSUS OBJECTIVES
Was the Objective Clear, Measurable, Achievable, Supports Future Picture?
1. Reconstruct Sequence of Events
2. Did We Accomplish the Mission Onjective?

A ANALYZE EXECUTION
1. Execution Errors/Successes
2. Cause of Each Error/Success
3. Identify Root Cause For Each Error/Success

Possible Root Causes		
Original Goals	Six Steps to Mission Planning	Task Saturation
• Leadership	1. Mission Objective	• Checklists
• Organization	2. Threats	• Crosschecks
• Teamwork	3. Available Resources	• Mutual Support
• Communication	4. Evaluate Lessons Learned	
• Discipline	5. Courses of Actions	
	6. Plan for Contingencies	

L LESSONS LEARNED
Prominent/Recurring Root Causes

T TRANSFER LESSONS LEARNED
Accelerates Experience
Improves Future Execution

Flawless Execution Model ℠
BRIEF
PLAN
WIN!
EXECUTE
DEBRIEF

H HIGH NOTE
Positive Summation

What are good times to debrief? You can debrief at the end of a shift, the end of a fiscal quarter, after a major sales call, after each game, after the release of a new product, after the gain of an important new piece of business (or in the wake of a loss), after the close of the store, after the change of inventory—in all of those natural moments that define the end of a cycle in your particular business.

S: SET TIME/LOCATION/PREPARATION

Whatever your cycle, the best *time* to debrief is when information is still fresh. Fighter pilots go into their debrief exactly forty-five minutes after they land. They get out of their jets, do their housekeeping, then arrive at the debriefing with their onboard radar and Heads-Up Display (HUD) tapes cued and their notes ready; they close the door and have a formal debrief for a precisely defined period of time.

As *you* prepare for your debrief, set the time and tell people what to bring. Disseminate key information to everyone so that all the participants have a clear expectation of the objectives, the process, and what they need to have in hand. Critical information required:

- **Time.** Set the date and start and end times. Start on time. End on time. Because STEALTH is a seven-step process, have a start/stop time for each step.
- **Location.** Set the location. You must have an environment that will enhance open communication as well as limit distractions. It doesn't hurt to have a room designated for debriefs. In fighter aviation, there's just one room used for debriefs, and we know it. When they walk in, they're debriefing.
- **Participants.** Define participants—the exact shift, department, or project team. No excess personnel allowed—only the people involved in the project—but no MIAs. We want all of the people on the team to debrief together.
- **Roles.** Clearly define everyone's roles:
  - *Leader.* This is not necessarily the senior person on the team but rather the mission leader. Why? This is the same person who led the brief. This is the person who's ulti-

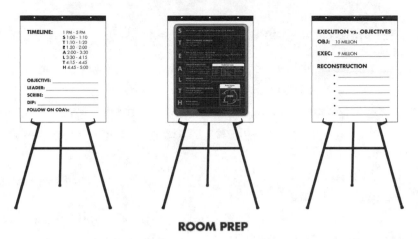

ROOM PREP

mately held responsible for the outcome of the mission. The debrief leader is the mission leader.

- *Timekeeper.* This person keeps the team on the proposed timeline throughout each step of STEALTH.
- *Scribe.* You'll be using whiteboards, so you want someone with legible handwriting to put data on the whiteboards as you progress through the debrief.
- *Data input person.* After the debrief, this person will collect, analyze, finalize, and disseminate the debrief data.
- **Future steps.** Everyone is accountable, but who does what? Here is a detailed list of follow-up courses of action:
  - *Objectives.* Define objectives—what objective or objectives are you debriefing, and what future actions are desired? Most of the time you are debriefing with the aim of finding ways to do things better, or, if you did them brilliantly, passing the good stuff along to others— transferring lessons learned and changing future plans and/or strategy.

Let everyone know what they need to bring to the debrief. For example, if you are analyzing market share objectives, marketing may have to generate some analytical numbers.

- *Prep.* Prepare the room. Have a bank of whiteboards ready. Ensure that the room is clean and that it fosters a professional working environment. (See accompanying figure.)
- *Always start on time.* Even without all the participants. (Don't penalize the people who are on time; on the other hand, never allow the power of the debrief to shift to the late people.)
- *Always end on time.* Never allow the debrief to degrade into an endless postmortem. Unless the issue has particular vibrancy, when the stop time comes, stop.

T: TONE (NAMELESS, RANKLESS, OPEN COMMUNICATION; LEAD BY EXAMPLE)

It is absolutely critical that the debrief leader establishes a tone conducive to open communication. How do you do that? It's not about soft lighting or throw pillows. In the Air Force, as I walked into a debrief with my fellow pilots, we literally ripped the Velcro name tags off our flight suits and the ranks off our shoulders. That set the tone. We literally threw it all away as we entered the room and got down to business. That may seem sophomoric to you, but more than anything else that we did to set the tone, this symbolic act did it—we were there for a nameless, rankless debrief and we were open for good, productive, and sometimes tough, open communication.

Here's how you set the tone:

- **Nameless.** It really is nameless. With the exception of the leader, who starts the debrief with a list of his or her own mistakes (see more below), we used the third person during the debrief. Let's say that Gundawg, my wingman, was the second jet in the formation and he screwed up an alignment. In the debrief, I'd say, "*Number Two* was outside of the one-mile trail formation we briefed. *Two* needs to cross-check his position better." Gundawg, or George, or whatever his name or call sign is, is now reduced to the third person—he's just *Number Two*. That's powerful. It's impersonal. It's factual. No need to ruffle feathers. I never say, "*Gundawg,* you were outside the one-mile trail; you need to keep up with the rest of us." That's too personal, too direct; that's guaranteed to put Gundawg on the defensive, maybe put him on the other side of the table. No. Instead, I say it in the third person: "*Number Two* was outside the one-mile trail. *Number Two,* try to add a cross-check on your position."

Third person? It's invaluable. It is totally rankless. It opens communication. It bridges awkward situations. Often, a mission leader is a junior officer. In such situations, everyone is a senior officer. Number Two? A senior officer. But how much easier is it to highlight an error when you are not directly speaking to or about the person? Nameless. Rankless. *It's not who's right, it's what's right.*

- **Rankless.** It really is rankless. Turn the debrief around. What's the overall objective? Name a few things. To improve? To accomplish the objective? To stay alive? To earn a huge Christmas bonus? What do any of those objectives have to do with your position in the company? Not a thing. You may be a vice president but if you gloss over your mistakes, you're just another smoking hole in the ground, so take your rank off your shoulder. Get with the team. For the duration of the debrief, we are equals. No one pulls rank during the debrief. Pilots help each other in the air; they help each other on the ground. I don't care what your rank is when you're saving my life. That's the power of *rankless*. It builds teams. It leads to success.

- No fear of reprimand for highlighting our own errors or someone else's errors. However, maintain dignity and tact.
- Debriefs are based on facts, not opinions.
- This is a process, not a competition. The goal is to improve future execution within our organization, not to make ourselves look good.
- Only one person talks at a time.
- An easel will be set aside for the "parking lot rule." If a useful item comes up but it's outside the scope of the debrief, then we post it on an easel set aside for precisely this purpose. Those issues can be addressed elsewhere after the debrief—in the "parking lot."

How to Start

Just as the largely symbolic act of removing our name tags contributed to the tone, so too did our body language and the words we used in the opening minutes. The debrief leader was key. The leader reaffirmed the tone by standing in the center of the room and criticizing his or her mistakes first, *in the first person*. If I were the mission leader, I might have said, "I executed an unbriefed maneuver that caused our flight to get separated over the target area. I lost my focus." This is called *inside outside* criticism. Notice that I started in the first person. This is the only time we ever violate the third-person rule, but as you can readily appreciate, to be personal at the opening—to be direct and no-kidding—cuts through the tension like a hot knife through butter. Criticize first yourself (inside) and then go to your team for criticism (outside). Then revert to the third person.

Now wait for responses. Feedback is critical to a debrief but the first time you ask for feedback, be wary: The first person you call on may not really be open. They might make a soft compliment or a general point that is not particularly valuable to the debrief process. This is a great opportunity for you to push him or her—get them to throw that dagger right into your chest. Allow this phase to go on long enough to set the tone for all participants. Watch them closely; you will know when they are ready to proceed. The goal here is to establish the tone by taking the first dagger (and maybe even the worst dagger, if that's how the mission went). This is about opening the lines of communication. When you've done it, move on.

Inside/Outside

Starting *inside* reaffirms the importance of rankless debriefs. Imagine a newly hired member of your company. They're probably intimidated by the seniority of the debrief leader. They know this person controls hiring and firing and may even sign their paychecks. The new hire watches carefully. They're trying to read your body language, your tone. If you do it right, if you put out the right signals, if you communicate that you accept criticism and that you're open to critical communication, they'll get the message that a debrief is truly rankless, that an honest debrief is more important than anything else. That triggers a transformation. Suddenly, this newbie, this new hire, feels like a member of a team. They sense their value. They remember they were hired because they had *skills*.

146

And guess what—so do you. Imagine that! You hired someone be-cause they had *skills*. Ben Rothelsberger was a rookie in 2004, but when he was forced into the game and faced ten-year veterans he led the grizzled linemen of the Pittsburgh Steelers to twelve con-secutive wins. Guess what? He was drafted because he had talent. But he wasn't the senior man on that field. He was a rookie. A rookie! Rankless is powerful. It gets people up to speed and pushes them to start carrying their own load. Can you see it in action? Can you see how it goes both ways and works on so many levels?

Granted, this is no easy thing to accomplish within the con-fines of corporate culture. But think about it—if we can make it work within the rigid structure of the military, where rank and se-niority are *everything*, then it can work anywhere. The key is you—the example must come from the top. Failure to start at the top will invariably lead to a failed debrief. To the thousands of se-nior executives I've talked to over the years, I say this—this is *your* leadership challenge.

One more thing: Something I said earlier bears repeating. In fighter aviation, experienced pilots want their new wingmen to feel comfortable giving senior and junior pilots *directive* commu-nication in the air. What is this? Directive communication is sharp and to the point and has nothing to do with being polite and respecting rank. It's more like this: *"Missile on your tail; break left!"* It save lives. But how do you get a newbie to speak up when there's no missile on your tail but there is nonetheless a problem? A good way to start is the nameless, rankless debrief. Get the new people to speak up. They may save your mission or your life.

E: EXECUTION VERSUS OBJECTIVES

Now that you've got the team talking, move quickly to the funda-mental part of the debrief. How well did you execute based on what you said you were going to do? That's it. How well did you do? In this part of the debrief, focus on the results rather than the objectives.

First, start with these questions: "Did everybody understand the mission objective or objectives that we are debriefing? Was it clear in everybody's mind? Was it measurable? Was it achievable and obtainable? And, more importantly, did it support the overall Future Picture of this company?" These were the questions asked at the end of the mission briefing. Back then, the response was a roomful of head nods. But now it's different; the mission has just been flown. So ask again. If there's another roomful of nodding heads, great; the mission planning was well done and the objective was valid. No one has the right to use the brief itself as an excuse for a mission error. But, if there's disagreement and a bunch of confused looks, you have to open the floor to a discussion of the brief and/or the mission objective. If that happens, it is largely going to be about you. You will learn a lot about yourself as a leader, not always pleasantly, but that's what it's all about— improving. Reevaluate how you should change your brief or your objectives with the idea of getting your team to better focus execution against your desired strategy.

Next, go to the facts of the mission. Did the pilots hit the bridge—yes or no? If not, why not? Maybe the first bomb created a smoke field that blew over the target, obscuring it so that the second pilot couldn't see the object he was tasked to hit. All said and done, when the last jet departed the target area, the bridge was still standing. So what do fighter pilots do? In the debrief, they peel off the layers of the mission and identify facts. A missed target. A smoke field. Wind from the east. Obscured fields of vision. Bombs not on target. See it? If they debrief, maybe the next time out they'll hit the *downwind* span of the bridge first and the upwind span second, and the third jet will have a visual confirmation that the bridge dropped.

"Okay, Murph," a CEO might say, "do we debrief good results, or only bad results?" The answer is: You debrief all results. If Company X had a quarterly sales goal of $10 million and they achieved just $9 million, then the debrief will focus on the $9 million and try to understand why the revenues fell short. You're not focusing on the $1 million gap; that's obvious. You debrief the results—$9 million and you debrief the whole thing. Why did we fall short? Where were sales good? Where were sales bad? What have we learned?

The same holds true for *exceeding* a goal. If this company achieved $11 million in sales against a $10 million objective, they must debrief that success as well. Why was the objective so easily attained? Is the company about to break into a new level? Which product did best? Maybe this company was Apple Computers and they expected sales to come from computers, but debriefed and noticed that sales of the iPod were exceeding expectations. They debriefed so they had every reason to react: Put money behind the iPod and expect it to pay off. Do you see why you debrief success, too?

As we share our lessons learned throughout the company we improve future execution by precluding execution errors and by sharing execution successes. Both types of lessons learned have the same impact on the organization.

Finally, debriefs can be quite technical in nature. During fighter pilot debriefs, execution is reconstructed with the aid of video cameras and digital data from sensors on the practice targets. This technical feedback helps pilots determine exactly how they executed versus their objectives. You may have to reconstruct the elements of the execution to determine a mission's success or failure. What data needs to be part of your debrief?

ANALYZE EXECUTION

Now, let's analyze the data. You were able to draw out from the team what the facts were. You probably had a vigorous discussion. The results are now displayed in a linear fashion left to right on large whiteboards or easels. You've given each success or error its own whiteboard. Now, one by one, list the probable causes. What are the *root causes*?

Causation

The hardest part of a debrief is the art of determining a cause. A good place to start is this: What is a legitimate *cause*? A cause is always a *how*—and the "how" is always an *active human error*. Let's say that during this mission the squadron lost an F-15. How? It ran out of fuel. How? The active human error was that the pilot did not monitor his fuel state and did not abort the mission at the bingo (empty) fuel mark. That was the human error.

Every cause has a human component. The members of the squadron don't yet know why this pilot ran out of fuel, but they do know how. The pilot failed to monitor his fuel state according to the brief. Now they need a *why*. Yes, airplanes are going to run out of fuel, but if they run out of fuel when they're not supposed to, there was a human error involved. Think about it. But why? Why the error?

Only on the rarest of occasions will the "why" of a problem come down to personal negligence—a single person doing a terrible job. *People errors are the exception, not the rule.* More often than not, *organizational processes, organizational behavior and system failures* are the true culprits. Look at this in macro terms. An individual may have made an active human error, but what specific organizational process, organizational behavior, or system failure contributed to that error? What was the cause of that error? The answer is found through what we call *root cause analysis.*

Root causes are big things, systemic things. They're usually hard to see—and often not analyzed—because they're largely latent issues. Something about the culture of the organization or the training or the attitude may have contributed to the cause. These things are hard to see. To find them, we use two approaches: We look for a possible breakdown in the Flawless Execution cycle, or, we use an analysis tool we call LOTCD.

Using the example of the F-15 that ran out of gas, the squadron would analyze the error as shown below.

Was the root cause:

- Leadership?
- Organization?
- Teamwork?
- Communication?
- Discipline?

Leadership

Let's say that in this pilot's squadron the leadership subtly created a maverick attitude about fuel management. In fact, the squadron commander always came back with a warning light blinking in his cockpit, indicating low fuel. Other pilots picked up on this, which led subconsciously to a practice of stretching their fuel—in fact, it led to a feeling that they weren't tough enough if they *didn't* stretch their fuel. Countless pilots in the squadron landed with the warning light blinking and the female computer voice known as Bitchin' Betty saying "low fuel" in their helmets. Over time, well . . . they became numb to it.

In time, this leadership error came home to roost. Maybe bad weather delayed the mission. Maybe it was an imperceptible matter of minutes—*minutes*! Whatever the circumstance, the cause was leadership. The pilot heard the warning signal for low fuel, was probably conditioned to ignore it, and, with horror, finally realized that the sudden deceleration of his jet was terminal—he was out of fuel. It wasn't the pilot; it was an organizational issue. In this case, they'd probably have to get rid of the commander.

Organization

The flight leader briefed the team late (he was disorganized) and didn't cover fuel contingencies. In turn, the flight members stepped to their jets late, which caused a late takeoff. Trying to make up time in the air, the leader took off with full power, causing everyone behind him to tap into their afterburners just to catch up. This in turn caused the trailing flight members to have less fuel than the leader. The last pilot was doomed from the start—he started his mission low on fuel. He had no chance. Not his fault. The disorganized flight leader triggered a hopeless chain of events.

Teamwork

Let's say that this was a flight of four aircraft. Unforgivable. There were three other pilots who could have helped get the flight organized. Any of the pilots could have spoken up on the radio to alert the leader of an unsafe situation developing around fuel. We call this Cockpit Resource Management, or CRM. Pilots on a mission have to act as a team.

Communication

This is obvious. Anyone could have broadcast a fuel state.

Discipline

At any time, any of the flight members could have said "Stop." They all launched with the same fuel; they were all getting low. But none of the pilots had the discipline to say, "Abort, low fuel." Discipline.

Perhaps the cause can't be found in LOTCD. Then what? Now is the time to search for causes against the Flawless Execution cycle. Was the error a breakdown in one of the four phases?

- Was there a flaw in one or more of the Six Steps to Mission Planning?
- Was the brief confusing or imprecise?
- Was task saturation an issue? Were checklists, cross-checks, or mutual support used to mitigate task saturation?
- Debriefs? Had there been a lack of prior debriefs or effective debriefs preceding the mission?

Analyzing the Flawless Execution cycle can be invaluable. Maybe not everyone understood the mission objective, or the threats, or what kind of assets we had in play to help us win. Maybe we failed to identify all of our available resources, or maybe we didn't spend enough time on step six, the contingencies. What went wrong? Let's say there were five SAM sites around a target—a SAM trap, as they call it. But let's also say that they briefed only one SAM site around the target. That is a deadly difference. The pilots can neutralize one SAM site, but a SAM trap? SAM traps are incredibly deadly. They can't notch away to break the lock of one missile without being acquired by another. They turn away from one, are acquired by the second, and turn away only to be acquired by the third. So they ran into a SAM trap and lost an F-15. They briefed a solo SAM site; they ran into a trap. That is a catastrophic failure in the intelligence briefing, not a pilot error. That's the *why* of the error on this mission. The cycle broke down.

Capturing Data

Now is the time to pay close attention to how you capture data. It does matter how you write data on the whiteboards. (See the accompanying figure, cause/root cause analysis.)

Here is how fighter pilots squadrons do it: First, put just one success and one error on each whiteboard. Next, write down the active human error—the *how*. Next, use LOTCD, and/or the Flawless Execution cycle to identify possible root causes—the *why*. When asking *why*, brainstorm multiple root causes. Unlike the cause or the *how*, in the root cause dissection you will find multiple possibilities. (Under cause there will be only one.)

Now you have a room filled with whiteboards standing shoulder to shoulder; errors and successes arrayed left to right, one to a board.

Step back and look at your boards. Notice any patterns?

RECURRING ROOT CAUSES

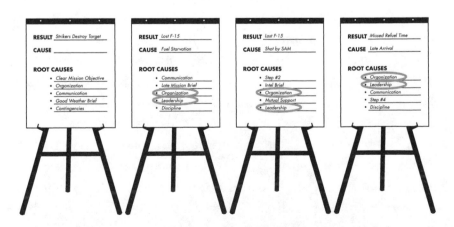

154

The Wheels Fell Off

Understandably, when a wheel came off a car during a test drive on a company track, the quality control department of this major auto manufacturer asked a lot of questions. How on earth did a wheel fall off? They determined the active human error was that the lug nut was improperly tightened. But, as they dug deeper, they kept asking why? Why was the lug nut not tight enough? *Because the tool was used at the wrong setting.* Why was that? *Because the person who usually did that kind of work was sick and someone covered for him.* Why was that? *Because the person who was sick had not communicated that he would be sick and a backup was not properly trained.* How could that not have been anticipated? The final answer was that there was not a standard operating procedure for that step on the production line.

Rarely is an error caused by a person. People are usually little more than the unwitting symptoms of organizational problems.

L: LESSONS LEARNED

Now it's time to look for patterns. In other words, we're looking for a *prominent* or *recurring* root cause that bridges together several errors or successes. It doesn't happen all the time. But if we find such a thing, take note: We have a significant problem (or opportunity). If we have an opportunity, we identify a way to get the message across the organization. If we have a problem, we identify a fix. The fix is what we call a *lesson learned.*

A lesson learned is not something small. Yes, there are plenty of glitches that surface in a mission debrief, and you learn from your analysis of these glitches and help each other, but a lesson learned is bigger than that. A lesson learned comes out of a pattern of *recurring* root causes. Here's a simple test. How do you know if you have a lesson learned? Ask yourself this: Should it be disseminated across the entire organization? Should the entire company (or department) change the way it does things because of the problem we've identified? If your is answer yes, likely you have a lesson learned.

As an example, let's look at a major sales call. Let's assume that a salesman is having trouble closing the deal. That's a legitimate issue, and you can help that salesperson improve. But it's worse than that. Let's say three or four salespeople had trouble closing. Guess what? That's a recurring root cause. That's a major problem. The entire company needs to do something *fast*. Maybe it's time to retrain everyone on closing skills. Maybe the company needs to create a checklist on the proper steps to closing a sale. Either way, the problem was a root cause problem and the fix goes up the organization to the CEO and down the organization to the training department. *That* is a lesson learned. One salesman is just one salesman; two identical problems with two different salesmen means there is a recurring cause. The proposed fix—retraining the sales force on closing skills—is a lesson learned.

Another example: the NFL. We know that after every game, the officials debrief. Let's say that after one particularly hard game they may have questioned how they were calling pass interference. Okay. But let's say that across the entire league there is a *pattern* of officiating errors related to pass interference. That's different. No longer is it *one* official or *one* bad day on the gridiron. Now it's a recurring root cause, and that requires a fix. The fix? Maybe they need something called an instant replay system.

Here's the message: A lesson learned is the result of a pattern of data points identified from the debrief that identify the root causes of an error that's being repeated and repeated and repeated. The fix has to be a change in the organizational processes, the organization's behavior, or the system. Think of this as something that affects your entire business silo, or your division (or you!) on a macro level. Identify what needs to be changed throughout the system in order to preclude future execution errors. That is a lesson learned.

A note of caution: Don't overdo it. How often can a mistake be so fundamental that the entire organization has to change? Not often. So how do you know if your mission team's lesson learned is a symptom of a bigger problem? In fighter aviation, several flight leaders fly missions at the same time. Lessons learned on one mission may be identical to those on another mission. Flight leaders let their commanding officer know what these are, and he or she compares the lessons learned to those of other squadrons. If there is a true, systemic root cause, it becomes an organizational issue.

- Lessons learned are systemic issues.
- A lessoned learned is always turned into a process.
- The process is always communicated as a precise series of steps—or actions—to take.

T: TRANSFER LESSONS LEARNED THROUGHOUT YOUR ORGANIZATION

Always tell people what you've learned. It is not good enough to simply identify the lessons learned. You have to communicate it throughout the organization. The specific fix you recommend needs to be clearly written so that others within your organization can understand the issue and benefit from the solution *even if they were not there*. You have to get the lesson learned out of your isolated debrief and into the veins of the company. You have to transfer knowledge quickly and help accelerate everyone's learning experience.

Let's go back in history. In Vietnam, if a fighter pilot could survive his first ten missions, there was a good chance he would survive 100 missions and go home to his family. But the first ten missions were tough—most of the pilots lost were lost inside of ten missions. To survive long enough to go home, a pilot first had to get through those initial ten missions.

As it happened, some squadrons were more successful in those first ten missions than others. What the Air Force discovered was that some squadrons did the full-on plan-brief-execute-debrief process, but some did not. Those that did kept more pilots alive than those that didn't. It was learned that not only was debriefing vitally important but that communicating the lessons learned—accelerating the learning curve—was enough to give a three-mission pilot the tools and skills of a thirty-mission pilot. It was all about survival. And it was that simple.

Write out a lesson learned as if your fellow fighter pilot were sick that day and had no idea of what went on during the mission or in the debrief that followed. Presume the reader is a rookie. It has to be that transparent.

Be specific. I can't fly my jet by a lesson learned called *organization*. I need a step-by-step process to implement that lessoned learned when I fly tomorrow.

In Business

At Afterburner, we want learning experiences transferred throughout our organization as quickly as possible. We have teams on the move every day of the week. Thus, after every seminar, no matter where they are, be it in Australia, the United States, or Europe, our main speakers and facilitators debrief following the STEALTH process. We post small lessons learned on our company intranet, and everyone in the company logs on daily to update themselves.

At the end of the year, the lessons learned are evaluated by a group charged only with the job of evaluating input from the teams. Those that are seen as true lessons learned are incorporated into our standards guide.

H: HIGH NOTE—POSITIVE SUMMATION

You have to end the debrief on a high note. Just as tone was set in the beginning of the debrief, the leader must set the tone again at the end. Debriefs are tough love; end it with love.

After dissecting a mission, admitting errors, and underscoring successes, you have to end the debrief with something positive. Did you take out the target? Say so. Despite a number of problems, did the mission end as briefed? Say so. Even if you ended the mission with a moderate fiasco, at the very least you can point out the fact that the debrief process is positive and that it's helping the group execute better in a rapidly changing environment. Always end the debrief with an honest, positive assessment of the team's execution. Nothing contributes to failure more than hang-dog faces. Send your pilots out on an up-note.

COMPLETING THE CYCLE

How does one put debriefs into proper perspective? As I said, it is at once our critique, our training, our intelligence gathering, the transfer mechanism for lessons learned, the catalyst to accelerate learning experiences, the foundation for the next mission brief—it's all these and more, with endless eddies spinning off into other disciplines. Lessons learned get passed up or down the execution engine from the associate level to the leadership ranks or down to the training level by keeping the managers in the loop after each mission cycle. This high tempo gives the managers time to make adjustments in their plans on an almost daily basis using the feedback from their direct reports.

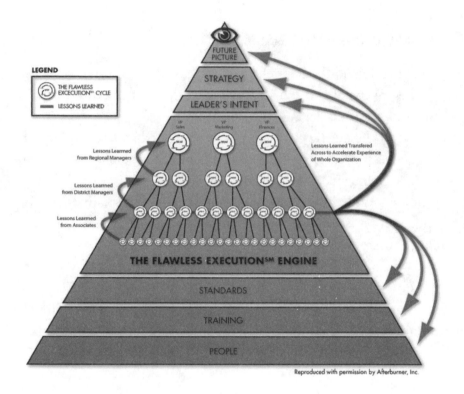

Reproduced with permission by Afterburner, Inc.

Standards

Reproduced with permission by Afterburner, Inc.

At the beginning of this book I was quick to define what I meant by Flawless Execution. Is any mission entirely flawless? Not at all. In fact, as I said, you give up a lot of points on the way to winning a basketball game—and every mission in my F-15 had a glitch, however small. But each mission improved the next because of the Air Force's unique processes for accelerating our learning experiences. In the aggregate, we started to outperform the competition—outfly the enemy—because our process had one unmovable aiming point, which was, of course, Flawless Execution.

But what happens when the plan breaks down? What happens when we're not there? Let's face it, we can't control everything. We can't be everywhere at once, and we sure can't do it all ourselves. The answer is standards. When the plan breaks down, you need standards to fall back on. If you're not around, if you've been shot down, if bad weather has killed all the phone lines, you have to know in your gut that your people have at the very least a strong set of standards to keep them performing their mission. You have to be able to rely on a minimum level of execution no matter how inexperienced a person is or how bad a handoff might be or how incommunicado you've become. You have to be able to rely on a minimum level of execution based on standards alone.

Now, let's dispose of some common confusion. Standards are not the same as compliance. Often, when I introduce this concept to companies, I hear back: "Murph, we have *rigid* standards—FDA food labeling, EOOC, FTC emission standards. We've got standards!" No you don't. You're confusing standards with compliance. Compliance is part of your environment.

Equally true, standards do include, but mean a lot more than, dress and etiquette. At our company we indeed have dress and etiquette standards. Our manuals spell out what everyone wears when they're traveling and when they're training, down to the color of their T-shirt under their flight suit (it's black). We also have etiquette standards. We answer our phones in three rings and always greet the caller professionally. But inside the Flawless Execution Model, standards are different things. They are the things that allow you to keep the mission alive even if, like Apollo 13, you've had a tank explode, you lose your electricity, and it's freezing cold in the capsule.

If a fighter pilot showed up in my squadron, I knew they'd been trained the way I was trained and I knew they had a core set of standards. Moreover, I knew this pilot had the discipline to carry out the process, to prosecute the standards, to fall back on good training. Why? We'd all been through this process ourselves, and we knew that he or she didn't make it to fighters by adhering to anything less. Our core standards were so well understood throughout our entire force of thousands of pilots that even in times of the unusual, unanticipated, one-in-a-million unscripted moment when we came face to face with a life-or-death situation for which we had no training or no scripted response, we could fall back on our standards. We could trust people we didn't train, we could trust people who had worked with us before; we could trust them to function because we all knew the standards.

Let me give you an example. One of my partners and one of our key main speakers is both an executive at Afterburner and an F-16 fighter pilot. On September 10, 2001, he was finishing a seminar in upstate New York. As it happened, the nearest airport was actually in Vermont. His seminar ended the afternoon of the 10th. He had another seminar on the 12th, so he spent the night in Vermont, planning to fly from Burlington to Houston, Texas, the next morning, the 11th.

The night passed uneventfully and he made his flight with time to spare. He boarded and sat on the airplane finishing up his paperwork. A little before nine, his plane started to taxi out to the runway at Burlington International when, several hundred miles away, on a morning few of us will ever forget, terrorists crashed a jetliner directly into the World Trade Center. Air traffic control shut everything down; everybody—all the traffic across the nation—was put on ground hold.

Well, my partner had no idea why he was sitting in this airplane in Burlington, Vermont, not moving, when around him there was no traffic. I mean, it's just cornfields and mountains up there. So he called me because he was afraid he was going to be late for the seminar. He said: "Hey, Murph, I just want to let you know our plane's running a little bit late, and you might want to call the client."

At first I didn't get it. I thought he was kidding. Didn't he know what had happened?

"Do you know why your airplane's late?" I asked. And then, while I was sitting there on the phone with him, the second plane hit the World Trade Center. Not believing my own eyes, I lowered my voice and told him what was happening.

Needless to say, he was instantly alert. He got out of his seat, walked up to the cockpit, showed his airline ID, and said, "Hey, Captain. Do you know why we're on the ground hold?"

The captain said, "No. We just got stuff on the ACARS (our internal communication system from the home office to the flight deck), saying there's some kind of national emergency going on."

My partner told the captain what had happened and the captain thanked him and asked him to keep him updated. They sat there for another hour and a half, in the airplane, locked on ground hold. Finally, they taxied back to the gate, and the passengers were let out.

Bolting off the plane, my partner immediately called his National Guard unit in Fresno and said, "Hey, California Guard. This is Major Bourke. What's going on?"

His commander said: "Get your tail here right now! We're manning twenty-four-hour combat air patrols over San Francisco and Los Angeles, and you've got to get here."

"Well, sir," he said, "I'm in Vermont. There's no way I can get there."

The commander didn't miss a beat: "Well, the whole air traffic control system's shut down. Go to the Vermont Air National Guard. They may need your help. *You're activated.*"

My partner said just two words: "Yes, sir."

So, here he was in his Afterburner shirt and his khaki dress pants and his nice shoes, and he had just been told he'd been activated. He rolled his bag over to a taxi and took a ride across the airfield, where the Vermont Air National Guard has its headquarters.

Dressed like an average Joe off the street, my partner walked up to the security guard at the gate and introduced himself. The guard, who by now had a slung M-16 and was at the ready, eyed him warily but he called the commanding officer, who is a general, and the general met him, right off the bat, right at the gate, and said, "Son, are you the Afterburner seminar guy that's stuck here?"

"Yes, sir, that's me, sir."

The general leaned closer. "You F-16 qualified?"

"Yes, sir," said my partner.

"Block Fifty?"

"Yes, sir."

"What size boots do you wear? I am short one pilot," said the general. "We need twelve pilots to man twenty-four-hour combat air patrols and I'm short by one; you're in a flight in two hours."

That was it. My partner walked right into a briefing room, stowed his wheelie, sat down, and introduced himself to everybody. The flight leader looked pretty grim and just said: "Sit down. The briefing's going to start." So he sat there, going through an hour and a half briefing, then suited up—and this California pilot launched in these Vermont F-16s with guys he'd never met before and flew for the next seven days, doing twenty-four-hour caps over New York City—one of the first jets on the scene.

How was that possible? Standards. Air Force standards are so thorough, the training so strong, that even though he'd never met these guys before, he got tasked right into the mission, basically had no questions, and went out and executed.

That's the level you need to have for those vitally important executional standards. Across your entire company, standards have to be set out so firmly, so clearly—and the employees disciplined so thoroughly to adhere to them—that even when you're not looking, the newest, greenest, youngest employee is at least executing his or her mission.

Now, I'll be the first to admit that getting there is anything but easy, but I also say that the rewards are incredible. One day I was in John Schnatter's office. If you don't know John, you should. John is the founder, chairman, and CEO of Papa John's International, Inc., the fastest-growing pizza company in the nation. He started Papa John's when he was a dishwasher in the back of his dad's lounge, Mickey's. When somebody didn't eat something, he was the guy who saw it because he washed and scraped the leftover food off their plates. It was as good as any research laboratory in the nation, when you think about it. He would see at all the food that people would return. So, after a while, he started figuring out what people liked and what they didn't like. Every now and then he would go to his dad and say: "Dad, people don't like the extra-spicy chicken wings. They eat the first couple, but they always come back loaded with the rest." One day he came to a realization that would change his life. "Dad," he said. "People never return the pizza. The pizza's always gone. I also noticed that people are particular about the crust. They don't touch it if it's soggy or too thick, but the pizza's always eaten."

All this gives him an idea. His *Future Picture* began to form. First, nobody ever returned pizza, so that's the right food to sell. Second, it had to be a thin, warm crust. Add that to a few other observations and you have a pizza business. He literally knocked out the wall in the back of the broom closet in his dad's tavern and started making pizza. That was the first Papa John's. He was in business. He was making and selling pizza, but more than that, because of his observations about what people liked and didn't like, he was actually making an excellent pizza, a remarkably good pizza—and his business thrived.

All these years later, Papa John's is now a system of more than 2,700 pizza stores. Better execution was on John's mind, which was why I was in Louisville, Kentucky, Papa John's corporate headquarters. As this was our first meeting, I asked John the question I ask of all our clients: "Where's your pain?"

John's answer stunned me. "My pain is that about 15 percent of our franchisees are underperforming. They thought they could buy a franchise and just sit back, and money would come in. They don't adhere to our standards. They want to sell chicken wings. They want to discount pizza. They want thicker-crust pizza. But we've told them this is how to make a perfect pizza. That's our business. This is how many tomatoes, these are the exact ingredients, and this is exactly what you sell it for. If you do that, you'll be successful. We know what works. But they don't follow the standards."

I was impressed. I'd never seen anybody as intense as this CEO. In fact, he wasn't finished answering my question. He was actually getting worked up. "It's a simple business, Murph. We make pizza. We're not flying F-15s with a Mig on our tails in weather upside down. We make pizza. And if you make it the way we tell you to make it, you'll have a healthy franchise. We rate our pizzas on a simple ten-point scale. We have statistical data that shows that if you're making a six-and-a-half pizza or above, you are going to have a profitable franchise. If you're making below a six-and-a-half pizza, you're losing money. It's standards, attention to detail. That's where we're dropping the ball. We've got the right system. We've got the right plan. We've got the pictures on how to make pizza. We've got Pizza University. We've put millions of dollars into perfect training. We've got great uniforms. We've got great stores. We've given our people every asset that they need, but our people don't get it. Just make perfect pizza. If you're making below a six-and-a-half product, I'm going to show you a franchisee that's underperforming and not hitting their numbers. If I show you a seven-and-a-half or above pizza, that's a franchise that's hitting their numbers. Our only mission in life, Murph, our *only* mission—forget about the training, everything else—our only mission is to make the perfect pizza. If we make the perfect pizza, we'll win this game. We'll win the war."

"John," I said. "What do you want to be remembered for? I mean, you've got the greatest team. You've got this beautiful building, up on the hill. You've accomplished everything you could ever want to accomplish at your age. What is it that you want to do?"

He thinks a second and says: "I want to be known for doing something better than anybody else in the world." He pauses. "And I think that is making pizza."

Let me tell you, he was shaking, he was so intense. I looked to his people and asked, "Have you ever heard that before?"

They said, "No."

Well, this is a man who goes to bed every night thinking about making the perfect pizza. He absolutely loses sleep when somebody down in Louisiana is making a six-point pizza. It took him years to figure this out. "We thought it was training for a while," he said to me as we left. "We hired the best training people in the world, and we put in training and software packages and pictures, but then we did this. Let me show you some pictures. That's a two and a half. That's a four and a half. That's a six and a half. That's an eight and a half. And that's a ten. Can you see a difference, Murph?"

I've never before in my life given the slightest thought to pizza, but I started looking at these pictures, and I could see his point. There's a big difference between a two and a half, with four pepperoni slices on this side and two on that side, and a "ten pizza," which was perfectly configured and had the right ingredients on it.

"If I put this pizza on your table and that pizza on your table, and there were ten people in the room, which pizza would go first?

I point to the eight and a half.

"Well, we've done focus groups, and that's exactly what happens."

Those are standards. If Papa John's can maintain a system-wide rating of six and a half or higher on their scale, they win the war. And it doesn't matter how smart someone is or what city they operate in or if the corporate office pays a lot of attention to the store owner personally; if you're a high-number operator, the people at Papa John's don't have to worry about you, don't have to mother you. They have standards. However many years it took to fine tune it, they did. They found the absolute minimum standard that, when all else is considered, points the way to be successful in the pizza business. Achieve that standard and you achieve your Future Picture—your Future Picture as a franchise that wants to make a buck, and Papa John's Future Picture to be the one pizza company that makes the perfect pizza.

We have several layers of standards at Afterburner, Inc. We have fifty-one different fighter pilot facilitators doing seminars all over the world, at all different times. Often, we'll have three seminars going on in three different cities on the very same day. But, despite the fact that all our team members are highly individualistic, extremely confident, well-respected fighter pilots accustomed to authority and command, when you see an IBM Afterburner seminar in Boston, and then another for Courtyard by Marriott in Florida, you'll see the same energy, the same high fives, the same plan-brief-execute-debrief-win message. We worked really hard to make sure that the environment is the same and the visuals and audio are jolting and high impact because we know how to deliver our message and we know what it takes to change people's lives. Our standards cut across every discipline. We want to ensure that everyone in the company is walking, talking, and chewing the Afterburner standards.

Just like Papa John's, we have a standards guide. In the same way that Papa John's pictorially shows a franchise what a perfect pepperoni pizza should look like, we spell out every thing we do and our standards for it. I remember our annual internal conference five years ago in Atlanta when we introduced it. "Guys, this is the standard. This is how you book your airfare. This is how you dress when you get on the airplane and when you show up. This is how you wear your flight suit, where your patches go, what color T-shirt you wear, where your name tag is. This is exactly how you hold your radios and what channel you'll be on. This is how you stand on stage. This is how you give a high five when a main speaker comes up on stage and takes your position. This is how you stand on stage when you're watching a videotape, looking at the screen, not at the floor, not at your notes, not getting some water, not walking around on stage, but at parade rest, military-precise."

When we hand that book to a new hire, they know what it means. This is the stuff that's going to save their tails in combat. In the fighter pilot community, if you know the standards, you pretty much can execute the mission without little idiosyncrasies tripping you up. Same with Papa John's. If you're not sure how many pieces of pepperoni to put on a twelve-inch pizza, just look at that photo on the wall. *"Never give a business card unless asking for one in return—ever. Always read the client's website and learn their language. Always show up prepared, line-up card in hand and ready to go."*

But, just like at Papa John's, getting people to follow the standards is a hard thing to do. We're human. We all want to do things our way; conversely, some people just won't go along. Maybe they're lazy, maybe they're uneducated, maybe they're just dreamers, but they don't, and soon enough those people have to go. But there's still that vast expanse of good people that mean to follow the standards but haven't yet fully disciplined themselves to do so. Those are the ones we work on and you work on. They have the potential; they simply need leadership. At first, I didn't do it all the time. Then I had to say, "If this is going to be our standard, then I've got to live the standard. I've got to set the example, have the discipline to adhere to it, and then hold our other main speakers to that standard." In our standards guide, it says, "As the main speakers, you're the on-site commanders. You are Afterburner. You are the standard." Now, I live and breathe what I expect everybody else to do—and rare is the day that anyone deviates.

As I said earlier, our standards cut across every phase of our operations. Every Monday, our operations team briefs and debriefs. We brief the week's mission. We debrief the previous week's mission.

Every Tuesday, our hunter team—our sales and marketing team—briefs and debriefs. If they're traveling, we have a one-hour phone bridge. Couldn't be simpler. Tuesday morning, no matter where you are, you're on the phone bridge—and no one misses it.

And then at the seminar, we have a briefing, too. For the larger ones, that can be an involved, detailed briefing. Anytime we have over 120 attendees, we have four or five facilitators. Our experience has taught us that when we have four or more facilitators, we need to designate a person as the "CINC SETUP." CINC SETUP is the on-site commander in chief who makes sure the room is set up properly. They make sure that the radios are all set to the right frequency so our people can move these large groups to and from the main session and the break rooms quickly and smoothly. They test the building for interference and work out a back-up plan to the primary radios. They check the large screen, the audiovisual system, and the sound. They communicate with the client to make sure that they have a breakout list and a roster of all the attendees. They make sure that the hotel concierge put up the pipe and drape in the right places. They make sure there's a cherry picker onsite so that when the seminar's over, we can pull our parachutes off the ceiling, pack up, and get to the airport.

Finally, that person is responsible for the mission brief. "We're going to start at eight o'clock. Here's the timeline. This is the order we will line up on stage in. Here's what's going to happen if, for some reason, Murph, the main speaker, talks five minutes over. We're going to slip the timeline here, and cut the break to ten minutes versus fifteen. This is what the primary radio frequency is. Here's what the backup is." Just like the mission briefs when I flew the F-15.

To give you an example of how useful this is in business, we can have an entirely new, *inexperienced* CINC SETUP do a briefing and never miss what needs to be covered because the entire briefing guide follows our standards.

Next, we always do a debriefing after the seminar, but we go another step with this: We post the lessons learned on our intranet. Our idea here is to transfer the lessons learned from every experience to all fifty-one members of our team, wherever they are in the world. To make that work, another standard states that everyone reads those lessons learned, weekly, as if they were actually at that week's seminar. This accelerates our learning experiences, as by now you know. Even if you're not doing a seminar that month, you can maintain your proficiency because you're reading the lessons learned of all the other seminars. Never personally been to a health-care seminar as a facilitator in our company? Just read the seminar debriefs under the keyword "health care" and all the lessons learned from the last three years of health-care-related seminars comes up on your screen. Read them and you are well ahead of the game before you show up and get briefed on the actual seminar that day. And if the lesson learned is powerful or important enough, we may change the standards guide to reflect this new best practice.

Can you see how useful standards are? Can you see how standards back up the ideals of the Flawless Execution cycle? It's like lacing your fingers together—the fit is perfect. You orient yourself toward Flawless Execution, but you also set basic standards for everyone to fall back on. Together, this keeps us aiming toward that immovable object, but not at expense of becoming a smoking hole in the ground. When the plan falls apart, we have a system in place to make sure that everyone is still making an eight-and-a-half pizza.

Standards extend into every aspect of your business. We have a rigorous process for hiring new facilitators, and it, too, is part of our standards manual. First, without exception, to even be interviewed, you have to be recommended by one of our teammates. Why is this? Our people know what we're looking for, what an Afterburner facilitator is. The perfect new team member is not the most tactical Navy, Marine, or Air Force aviator; the best stick in the squadron; or the hottest pilot. Yes, they have to be former fighter pilots, but more importantly, they have to be fighter pilots who can *relate* their tactical aviation experiences to a civilian, usually through the filter of their own business experiences (almost all of our facilitators have been or are involved in a business). Beyond that, they must be comfortable speakers who make eye contact, and they're usually happy people—you know the type. By nature, or because they still fly for the Reserves or the Guard, they must be physically fit.

Once you've been recommended to us, our operations officer interviews you. He looks at your resume and gets you on a telephone interview. Then, if you pass muster, you fly to Atlanta, where you meet a partner. First, we take you to dinner and have some drinks. Did the candidate wear appropriate business casual as briefed or did he or she come under- or overdressed? Did he or she have more than one or two drinks? Could we trust this person to dine with a *Fortune* 500 executive and represent us?

The next day the candidate is told to report to the office in business attire at 0800—not 0745 or 0801. Once they get to the office, they'll go through a business interview to test their basic business knowledge, and then they'll be asked to give two three-minute presentations. One will be on a subject with which they are very familiar, regarding their flying background, and the other will be on a business leadership topic. If you get a thumbs up, you go to your first seminar. This is important. We want them to see the show, to see the seminar with all the lights, noise, and visuals up there. Are they comfortable with that? Can they handle an audience this large? If so, we hand them our standards guide. "Know it cover to cover," we say, and then we fly them to their second seminar. We actually put them to work on this second trip. It's a part of our training cycle we call demo/do—demonstrate to the student what you want them to do, then have the student do it. In this case, they've read the standards manual and know what to wear, what to bring, and what the script is for their role in the meeting. We have them follow a facilitator, watch how it's done, and expect them to do it flawlessly on their third trip.

On your third seminar, you have an instructor flying on your wing, and you do it. It's a three-seminar checkout process. Make it through all three, and you're hired.

One of the hard parts about standards is that they take time to implement. In the ideal world, I'd hand out a standards manual and you'd be groomed perfectly on every trip after that. In truth, it takes time and repetition. A behavioral psychologist did some study and found that it actually takes ninety days for a human to really pick something up and make it part of his or her daily regimen. If you've never been a dental flosser and you're trying to floss every morning, if you try it here and there, it'll never become a habit, but if you give it ninety days, most likely, you'll change you behavior permanently. What was hard at first is now habit.

No plan goes off without a hitch or a flaw. That's the way it is. The competition is trying to beat you, the environment changes, the technology changes, a piece of equipment fails—things happen. What's important is to make progress towards the immovable goal, the beacon, the Future Picture. That takes standards.

When the plan breaks down, you need standards to fall back on. You have to be able to rely on a minimum level of execution based on standards alone. That's what Flawless Execution's all about. In a sense, standards bring you full circle—they are the ultimate contingency plan. You can count on them to keep the system working. You can rely on them for a minimum level of execution until you fix the problem.

Without them, you come to a complete halt.

Training

THE FLAWLESS EXECUTION℠ ENGINE

Reproduced with permission by Afterburner, Inc.

The foundation of everything is training. Say it again and again. Training is essential to Flawless Execution. Training is nothing less than the rock-hard foundation upon which Flawless Execution is built.

The business world has an argument with that. The CEOs say: "Well, Murph, we don't have time to train because we're living and breathing our mission every day."

I don't disagree. But they're missing the point. No time for training because you're living and breathing and flying your mission every day? My answer? "Well," I say, "we're pretty busy, too, you know. We actually call that combat." Then I lay it out straight: "*We even train during combat*, because every time we have a mission, even if it's a real, heads-up, no-kidding combat mission, we have our mission objective, we have our secondary objectives, and sometimes we even have DLOs—our desired learning objectives. Wars aren't won in one mission; war is a sustained campaign. And if we don't continually train during a sustained campaign, if we don't strive to learn, to brush up on our other skills while we're sustaining that campaign, we're never going to get better. Worse, if our missions are the same day in and day out, we may be letting some critical skills get rusty that might be called on tomorrow. If that happens, we're never going to get out of that unexpected problem that will kill us."

That's why there's always time for training, even on a combat mission during war.

If you're in it to win, if you're to transfer the concepts of Flawless Execution into a daily practice, you can't look at training as a problem. It isn't a hindrance. It doesn't get in the way. It *is* the way. You have to have training, and, believe me, you have to have ongoing training, even while you fly a combat mission.

Sometimes that answer isn't enough, though. I understand that. But there's another way to look at training, and it is salient to the pressing demands of the fast-changing, hypercharged world of business today. We don't quit training and you don't quit training. Your environment and my environment are changing so fast that it's hard to keep up, much less jump ahead. Everything in life is in a continuum, and that continuum is called *change*. If you're going to get ahead and win, you've got to be able to create change at a faster rate than the rate at which the environment is changing. Colonel John Warden, one of the planners of the Desert

Storm air campaign, said it best in his book, *Winning in Fast Time*: "You won't win in the twenty-first century by merely reacting to change or making incremental improvements to maintain your current position. To win, you must decide what you want your tomorrow to be, and then make it happen faster than the rate of change in your competitive environment" (John A. Warden III and Leland A. Russell, *Winning in Fast Time*, Venturist Publishing, 2002). How can you stay ahead of the rate of change if you're rusty on your basic skills? How can you stay ahead of the rate of change if you don't have any idea what your sales data mean? How do you counter the tendency to get soft, to relax, to ride on yesterday's skills? You train. You train just like an NFL football team trains. You throw 1,000 passes to that same wide receiver on that same route until the two of you can connect with your eyes closed. Dull knives don't cut. Rusty keys won't open locks. You train the essential life skills that you have to use in your competitive environment until you can complete that pass with your eyes closed. You study the competition (a form of training). You plan contingencies (another form of training). You practice your execution. And you repeat it and repeat it time and again until your skills are not only sustaining you but have you accelerating ahead of the pack.

That's the secret to real training. You sharpen the knife. You oil the pliers. And when your tools are at their peak performance, you often jump ahead of the pack. You turn faster, you react quicker to a missile, *and maybe you do something that no one has ever done before, and viola! You just jumped ahead of the rate of change.* I can't count the number of innovations that came from trained soldiers smart enough in their essential skills to leap ahead with an innovation that forever changed tactics. In World War II, a Marine Corps fighter pilot in the Pacific named Pappy Boyington came up with deflection aiming. Some soldier on the ground in France modified the tanks to break through the hedgerows. And, as amazing as it sounds, during World War II, someone actually came up with the idea of having a direct communication link between the ground forces and the air forces. It had never been thought of before! Preparation meets opportunity, and innovation is its birth child.

The reason our fighter pilots are better than any other fighter pilots in the world (and I'm not talking about technology—some of the new Russian technology is almost as good, if not better, than the stuff we have) is that our pilots are trained at such a high level.

People with sharp fundamental skills are invariably the catalysts. It's that simple. But there's training and then there's Training. So it should come as no surprise to you by now to learn that fighter pilots have a four-step process that accelerates training and maintains life's essential skills. That process is this:

- **Step 1:** DLOs (desired learning objectives)
- **Step 2:** Demo/Do
- **Step 3:** Discipline
- **Step 4:** Continuation Training

DESIRED LEARNING OBJECTIVES

In the Air Force, pilots are told that they're responsible for their own training. As an Air Force pilot, this was repeated to me time and time again. "You keep track of your book time and you keep track of your simulator time. You're responsible for your own training. If you're going to get better, you're training cycles will get better, but it's up to you."

One of the most effective ways to penetrate the brain and reach wherever it is that we store our experiences and actually learn is through hands-on training. Fighter pilots would start their training cycles with DLOs—desired learning objectives. My training officer would stand before me and say: "Go study this, Murph. This is how you do this maneuver—the Cuban eight. I want you to read about this tonight. Then, tomorrow, I'm going to come over to the squadron, and I'm going to brief you on how to do a Cuban eight. Then we're going to go demo/do."

Each block in our training begins with a DLO, and each DLO has with it a specific question: What do we want to learn today? What are the desired outcomes for today? The desired outcome may be to learn a Cuban eight or maybe how to navigate by compass alone or maybe how to lay sixteen pieces of pepperoni on a pizza. DLOs are very, very clear, measurable, specific desired learning objectives with exact parameters. The whole mission is built on one outcome—to learn it—and the whole debrief will focus on that outcome. "Did we meet our desired learning objectives in this area?" Yes? No? If not, why not?

Begin the training process like any mission: by stating a clear, measurable, achievable objective, and then executing your mission. In this case, execution may be to hit the books or to attend Pizza University or to rehearse a presentation before you stand before the client, but the secret of the learning process, the success ingredient in the fighter pilot's way of training, is to take it in steps, to take it one by one with clear, exact DLOs. Then, my friends, you do it, hands on.

DEMO/DO

After I'd studied the manual and understood the maneuver, the next step was to demo/do the maneuver. The training commander would probably stand up again and say to me: "I understand what the manual says, and that's what you think it means; but here's really why we wrote that. Let me *show* you." *Demo.* "I'm going to demonstrate the Cuban eight for you. I'm going to show you how to do it, and then I want you to do it. And we're going to do it over and over again. We're going to demo/do, demo/do, demo/do."

And I did that for a year, on every single maneuver. I read about it, I briefed it, I got it "demo-doed," and then I did it. I did it over and over again. And pretty soon, when I did these maneuvers 1,000 times over two years, out popped a fighter pilot. I hadn't been in an academic or theoretical training environment; I'd been doing things, doing them myself, touching the controls, feeling the G-forces, so when I had it down, I really had it down. My DLO was no longer something I had to think about. It became second nature. It was like an old glove.

How does demo/do work in the business environment? In many ways, big and small, as I learned the hard way. During the second year of Afterburner's being in business, I was speaking in front of 10,000 people in the Los Angeles Convention Center. We had a new software program. Our videos were streaming right off our computer hard drives so we didn't have to use separate VHS or beta tapes. Now, we always hire a local AV production company to handle the tricky timing of the audio CDs and the video images. This day was no different, but as it happened, things were rushed, and we were unable to do a compete dry run with the new outfit and with our new presentation software. Of course, the audiovisual company we hired tried to reassure me that they were professional and could handle the script and did this all the time. Well, we learned, even then, in our second year of business, that our Macintoshes are different from most PCs, and, a lot of times we have interface problems. That day we had just a ten-minute dry run, and right away we had interface problems. We got over that but the time was up so I handed the technician the script with his audiovisual cues and said, "Follow this."

Of course, the AV guy had five other presentations that day. He had his professional pride on the line, so he said, "Okay, great.

I'll just read the script. I do it all the time," and I walked out on-stage. Boy, did I learn to practice what I preach.

I followed a pretty famous comedian, and the whole place was just rocking and rolling. After thunderous applause and waves of laughter, he introduced us. He said: "Now, we're going to bring up some top guns, some real, red-blooded, American fighter pilots," and the anticipation he developed was intense. So, to our stirring music, I walked onstage in my flight suit. I was walking left and right before 10,000 people with images of F-15s and F-16s flashing behind me as I started my intro when all of a sudden the screen went *szchwew*! and a video segment not due for five more minutes started running. The AV guy misread the cues. It started playing in front of 10,000 people. I said over my microphone, "Can you hit the return button real quick and play that in just a minute?" This poor fellow hit return, and the whole program crashed.

Luckily, we always travel with a primary computer and a back-up computer, so we switched to the backup. The seminar went on without a hitch, but for three agonizing minutes, I was on the stage in front of 10,000 people with a video screen that was sputtering with almost nothing happening. I had violated my own rule of demo/do. My fault. But it was a huge lesson learned. No matter how rushed, always demo/do. That's the way training works in even the sharply compressed time frame of everyday business. You use the process even on a quick handoff.

Nowadays, I never hand anyone a script. Rather, I demo/do. I make them write down, in their own notes, in their own hand-writing, their own script. Yes, I get complaints all the time: "You don't have a script for us to follow? You know, a timeline, or anything with your slides or pictures?" I say no. In fact, it's our standard to say no. Demo/do, right? I want them to look at the script themselves, and I want them to write down, in their own notes, with their own words, what to do when, and I want them to visualize the presentation. Then I have them advance slides and trigger some AV. That's how you train on the fly—train even in the middle of the workflow. You fall back on the process. They have to take my presentation and make it theirs. I have to make that happen. Demo/do works best. You can't do it any other way. Demo/do.

Training is an art. You can tell people all day long how to do something, and they can read about it and study it, but they have to live it. You have to put the paintbrush in their hand. They have to sit down in front of the computer and work their way through the commands until they've mastered the new reservation system or the new CRM software. They don't watch. They have to do. And then, when they've got it mastered, they have to have the discipline to use it.

DISCIPLINE

The third step in training is discipline. In our model, *discipline* is the discipline to carry out the process, to prosecute the standards, to fall back on good training. I'd have assumed you're trained and you're a killer if you showed up at my squadron. But would you have the discipline to execute within the standards of *our* squadron? Maybe we found out that operating in the Middle East is little different from operating in North Carolina, and you're from North Carolina but we're about to redeploy to the Middle East. With the experience of squadrons that have deployed before us, we have a set of standards and they're different from your home base's squadron standards. We've all been trained the same way and we're all in the same company. Would you be disciplined enough to fly in my squadron with my standards? Could you stay on the process? Could you stay on the plan? If you didn't have that, then you couldn't move on to the next level.

Have you ever heard the term *gold-collar employee*? An article in the *Harvard Business Review* first brought this concept to my attention. Gold-collar employees are not senior executives; rather, they are the absolutely essential, must-have employees who keep your business running. These are the men and women who staff the front desk in a hotel or drive the delivery trucks or handle the baggage. In the world of a fighter pilot, they are the refuelers, maintainers, weapons loaders, and life-support people who make sure the G-suits are functioning properly.

Gold-collar employees are the people without whom you can't run a business. They are worth their weight in gold by being there (versus a golden parachute employee, who is one you've jettisoned yet makes money on the way out). But what makes them valuable? First, they have the training to get the job done. More importantly, they have the discipline to do their jobs. They show up on time, they drive their routes, they care about the customer, they adhere to the standards—and they have the will to do their jobs exactly how you want their jobs to be done. That's an employee who parks in the employee-of-the-month spot.

Do you have the same discipline as these must-have employees? Or, said another way, are you setting the standard and living your corporate discipline? Once again, I learned the hard way just how important that is to the process. While everyone at Afterburner knows our standards guide cold, in the early years our people were getting mixed signals. It was me. Maybe it was just here and there, but on more days than I care to admit, I was relying on others to pick up the pieces. Most obvious to all—my attire. I wrote the standards on attire, but I was cutting corners. If you want your people to wear business casual, then you better wear business casual. If you want your training to take hold with your new people, then you have to see to it that what's written in the guide is acted out by you. If you wear jeans, you undercut the discipline. If you wear a coat and tie, you undercut discipline. Discipline means you do exactly what is asked of you. You don't undershoot the standard; you don't overshoot it either. You hit it on the nose. And for it to work company-wide, that starts at the top.

CONTINUATION TRAINING

Once a year, we fly everybody to Atlanta, and we have a two-day standards seminar. All we do is focus on our standards. We know that it takes exactly forty-one minutes for our main speakers to go through the task saturation keynote, and we know our facilitators have forty-one minutes to get through a STEALTH debrief. Our content, our pacing—everything's been refined over nine years and is down to a science, one that's been developed and modified before over a million participants. We know what works and what doesn't, what gets the message through and what distracts. But we never take for granted that all fifty-one of our people are staying current. It's the old 100-80-80 rule. As the leader, I have 100 percent of the knowledge and enthusiasm and dedication, but the person under me can at most have just 80 percent of that knowledge, enthusiasm, and dedication—and the person below that, only 80 percent of the person above him. It dilutes quickly. So we have our recurrency training, our continuation training, our two-day seminar, and we make sure that everyone is up on the dress codes, up on the content and has the pacing down cold.

Continuation training is secondhand to pilots and to many other professionals, including lawyers, doctors, and accountants. In our field, and each of theirs, staying fresh, keeping up with the changes in their professions, is so important that continuing education courses are required by law. In truth, they should be required at every company, no matter what size. Maintaining the essential skills to fly a commercial airliner is no less important than maintaining the essential skills to sell a high-speed Internet connection. If your pilots can't fly, if your salespeople can't sell the basic service, you have no business. You're grounded. If you have an annual sales meeting, as most companies do, put aside a day for recurrency training, continuation training. Few of us can say that we couldn't do a little better by spending a half day fine-tuning our essential life skills.

Fighter pilots rate their experience on how many hours they have in the jet. They know they're not in training command anymore; they're in the F-15. They're frontline fighter pilots now. Every hour in the F-15 puts them higher and higher and higher in that level of experience and training. The more hours they have, the sharper and broader their skill sets.

High-time pilots get no slack. They train, they have recurrency requirements, and they have the same standards as the new hot stick on the block. But guess what? Those high-time pilots are the first in the briefing room, the first to criticize themselves, and the first to work the squadron ever closer toward Flawless Execution.

Training isn't something that gets in the way. Training is the way that gets you there.

People

"Get the right people on the bus, in the right seats."
—JIM COLLINS, author of *Good to Great:*
Why Some Companies Make the Leap . . . and Others Don't

Reproduced with permission by Afterburner, Inc.

I hear this comment so frequently I can repeat it in my sleep: "People are the most valuable asset to our company."

I think that's exactly right, but rarely do companies put much thought into the *people* process of the company. Don't get me wrong. I fully understand that an entire industry has grown around tools to help companies screen employees better. But there is still something missing.

I first realized how important this is as I was finishing my F-15 training at Luke Air Force Base in Arizona. At this point in my military career I had been in the Air Force just eighteen months and flying jets for a grand total of just 280 hours. I had passed my initial flight screening; survived jet school, or UPT as we called it in the Air Force; made it through our high "G" training in the centrifuge; graduated from fighter pilot lead-in training; survived combat land survival and water survival; and was finally sitting at the top F-15 school, where only the best are invited in. What struck me was that each man in my class came from a different background, a different part of the country, and a different educational system, but we were all incredibly similar. We all dreamed about the same things, laughed at the same jokes, drank the same type of beer, talked in similar patterns, had similar mannerisms, and chewed gum the same way. Most importantly, we were all getting paid about $24,000 a year to risk our lives on a mission objective that someone else had written. The attention to detail, the esprit de corps, camaraderie, and overall quality of this group was impressive, and *we were working for the government!* How in the world did this happen? Would you like to have such a team in your organization?

It was no accident. The Air Force knew exactly what it took to be a fighter pilot. It knew the character traits, the cultural background, the physical and psychological traits required to excel in the cockpit of an F-15 or F-16.

Most companies don't have more than fifty years of experience understanding the unique requirements for a job function that has remained relatively constant for five decades. Sure, our planes are magnitudes faster today than they were in 1947 and the cockpit load twice that, but the basic job is the same. Fly a mission; get back alive.

In order to get a pilot slot in the USAF I had to pass a basic aptitude test, a rigorous physical exam, a psychological profile, and a test that looked at my eye-hand coordination, spatial memory (how well do you operate in a multidimensional environment), and basic aviation knowledge. This was just to get in the door! Then I had eighteen months of high-intensity training with plenty of opportunities to wash out before I arrived at an F-15 unit. Why did the Air Force invest so much in assessing us? Because it takes over $6 million to get an F-15 pilot trained and ready for combat.

How much does it cost your company every time one of your employees doesn't work out? Lost training costs, travel, an investment in your staff's time, lost productivity, and the all-important lost opportunity costs. Dr. Brad Smart, the author of the book *Top Grading*, studied more than fifty corporations and found out that it costs an average of fourteen times a person's salary for a miss-hire in the $100,000 range and twenty-eight times the salary in the $100,000–$250,000 range! Smart goes on to say that 50 percent of all employment situations result in a miss-hire.

Look at your organization. Do you know what qualities it takes to excel in your own environment? Not the skills your business requires, but the character and culture it will take to be successful in your unique environment. At Afterburner, we screen new employees rigorously, and we're so good at it that we developed assessment tools our clients can use when they screen prospective employees. But there is so much more to it than that. People can fake their way into the wrong job. You can talk yourself into a bad hire. No, what you have to do is be forever mindful of that vague, nebulous thing called "fit." In the end, does a person fit your corporate culture?

In the business of training companies, culture is something we see firsthand. Marriott wants engaging, outgoing people at the front desks of the Resident Inns. When I spoke to more than 600 of them, I was struck by how similar they were—well-groomed, happy people who seemed more interested in me than in themselves.

Southwest Airlines is well known for its unique culture. They want people who like to work with each other. Get through the gate at Southwest and you'll probably see a few photos from the last Halloween or birthday party. This is a company that likes to have a little spirit rub off on its customers—after all, the airline may be no frills, but it doesn't cost any money to laugh.

Accountants probably don't need to laugh all day, but they do want a culture that matches their interest in accounting. Would it be appropriate to transfer Southwest's culture to an accounting firm? Probably not.

That's part of the Air Force's secret. I had to pass a lot of written tests, but I also had to shake a few hands and have a few dinners with the guys in the squadron. Those dinners were about culture—would Jim Murphy fit in?

In my previous book, we discussed setting the bar high in order to create an elite team in which only the top performers are attracted. One only has to look at special forces teams like the Navy's SEALS to see the top-notch talent they attract. The point is this: It is not always about the best compensation package or the benefits you offer but the pride and self-satisfaction you get by being part of a special team. Good companies make their people into exceptional workers. Exceptional workers execute better because they have something more at stake than themselves—they have their peers, their culture, the approval of those around them. In companies that bring the right people together, however the process, those factors lead to Flawless Execution.

Individual Execution

Up until now, we've dealt with the art of Flawless Execution from the larger, corporate perspective. The leadership develops a Future Picture that then translates into strategies through open planning, which is then fed into the execution engine. But what about small companies and small teams? What about *you*? More times than I care to remember, entrepreneurs and small business owners have come up to me and said: "Murph, I'm too small to make this work." They worry that they have to have a large company mentality and, even more daunting, a large corporate pocketbook to achieve Flawless Execution.

Nothing could be further from the truth, but I understand their point. Small business is the backbone of America. In a small business, resources are lean, money is precious, and no one has enough time—kitchen remodeling companies, lawn and garden services, print shops, small accounting firms, retailers of all sorts. Pick one: Everyone is busy; money is precious. "What resources do I have to spend on anything other than running my business?" they ask. "Isn't there enough to do just to get by?"

All the more reason to pay close attention, because in a small business, mistakes have a disproportionately higher impact on the company than they do in a large corporation. Now you're in a world where one flawed mission can be crippling and instantly spin uncontrollably into a death spiral. Things are extraordinarily "real" in a small business. In a large corporation, you might be able to lose control of the finance department for a few weeks or suffer a cash flow crunch, but in a small business, that cash flow crunch can feed instantly into vendors who won't ship, creditors who won't wait, and a healthy company suddenly unable to pay its bills. A prominent, thriving small business can be gone in mere months. I know. I've seen it happen and so have you. There's no buffer, no "department" to hide in.

Then there's the logic-proof compartment inside the head of every small business owner that I've ever met. No matter how you say it, every small business owner thinks he or she has a unique set of problems that no outsider could possibly help.

Thankfully, Flawless Execution works in a small business, a home business, and in you. There's nothing about a "corporation" that's written into the rules. There's nothing about a fancy conference room or teams of executors that makes the Flawless Execution Model work. Quite the contrary. Flawless Execution is a bottom-up process, to change the way *one* person develops the Future Picture, *one* person plans, *one* person briefs, *one* person executes, *one* person debriefs. It's designed to help one person out of a tight corner, one person to sell better, one person to collect payables better, one person to do whatever they want in life better than anyone else. If you apply that to a small company, that helps that one small company grow and be profitable. As I've said before, corporate success is based on individual execution, whether you're a company of one or of 1,000. Remember the Army's most successful recruiting campaign in its history? An Army of One . . . You can be in meatpacking, beverage distribution, machine tooling—it doesn't matter. I don't care if your conference room looks more like a closet filled with cartons of supplies. Flawless Execution is a people process, not a corporate process. It works in me, in my team, in my squadron, and in the air wing. It works in you, in your people, and in your company. To illustrate, let me give you examples of Flawless Execution in two entirely unrelated but highly individualistic settings: marlin fishing and medicine.

Marlin fishing is different than normal fishing, because it's truly a team effort. You have the angler, who's cranking the marlin—a 1,000-pound fish—and the captain, who has to drive the boat. Because these fish swim at thirty-five miles an hour, and the boat is trolling at nine miles an hour, the fish can strip off so much line that driving the boat is key. The captain has to anticipate where the fish is going. If a fish runs and strips off 500 yards of line and starts turning, and if the captain doesn't anticipate that turn—let's say he's steering the boat in the wrong direction—he's going to run over the line or strip the fish off. That's a bad day in the charter business; worse in a marlin tournament.

But there's more. Once you get the marlin up to the boat, then the first mate has to lead the fish alongside—grab the leader and bring the fish in close enough without himself being yanked overboard and without breaking a line or pulling the hook out of the fish's mouth. Then a third person has to tag the fish because the only way you get credit for catching one of these things is to tag the marlin. And then there is an observer. The observer verifies the catch. "Good tag. Good release. You get 500 points." That's how they catch marlin. This is their sport and their game and they're deadly serious about it.

I'd never been marlin fishing until several years ago, but I decided to try it. I went down to Florida, found my charter, and got on the boat. There we were, the four guys on our angler team—a first mate and a captain, a tag-man, and me. We were all sitting there, and there were hooks around me—large ones, razor sharp—

and we had six lines going out the back of the boat through out-riggers, an intricate system. The boat was making its way through some hefty seas. Nothing happened for hours and hours and hours. I just sat there watching the lines and lures skipping across the water as the boat trolled along.

All of a sudden, one of those fish hit, the reel went off, and the line started stripping. It was going out so fast you could hear it sing. It was literally making the reel burn. The captain started yelling instructions. But me? I didn't know what to do. Everybody was screaming at everybody, and they were bumping into each other, people almost getting hooked with gaffs, almost getting thrown overboard. The fish came to the boat, and more people were screaming and yelling, and it was very dangerous. We were at sea with these huge waves—it was hard to even stand—and all this was going on. I was sitting there thinking to myself: "Wow. We should have had a briefing before we left the docks. Someone should have told me that if one of the reels went off, Murph, in the first half hour, you're the angler. I want you to get in the seat, and I want Ed here to help you strap in and then everybody else stay clear of the area. When the fish gets here, only the first mate goes forward. And when he touches the leader, nobody else talks. Angler can't talk; captain can't talk. The first mate will be in charge of the whole situation."

But, of course, I'd been told none of this before we shoved off despite the fact that marlin fishing is incredibly dangerous. If I'd accidentally put my arm back and hit the tag man—who's got this sharp pole that pops the tag onto the fish—I'd get tagged!

But why should it be like that? The next night at the docks, I gave them a talk about Flawless Execution. I told them what it was like sitting alert in an F-15 squadron when the horn went off and the other pilots had to scramble. We went from dead sleep to a flat run, jumped into our jets, strapped in, looked over these 350 instruments, started, taxied, and pushed up the throttles to full afterburner and got up into the night sky all in less than five minutes to find that bogie. You think that's not dangerous? Moreover, the maintainer and the weaponeers went from a dead sleep, and all of those people were scrambling around our jet, too. In that world, everybody had to know their position because, if they didn't, somebody was going to get sucked up into a jet intake.

So, I talked this out with the marlin people. Just like my F-15 squadron, or better yet, just like on an aircraft carrier, we needed to think about this and think about that and have a plan and brief it before we took a marlin charter out to sea because, once we are out to sea, it's rough, and people are getting sick, and things are happening fast.

The captain was listening to me, so I went on. "If somebody had just told me 'the boat's going to do this and we're going to react this way while you should do that,' I wouldn't have been sitting there thinking, 'What's everybody doing? Am I in the way? What should I do?'" As a novice, my situational awareness (SA) was nil. Even a short briefing would have pushed my SA much higher and the experience would have been better and I might have gone back for another charter. As it was, all I saw was chaos (fighter pilots hate chaos), and I told them I wasn't certain I wanted to do it again. Life's too short—recreation is not supposed to kill me.

Can you see the gaps, the holes, the absence of any structure—much less any feedback—that allowed years of bad habits to perpetuate? Can you see how strange crew members will start bumping into each other, unsure what the standards are, or how novices will walk away from their one experience of marlin fishing with lessons learned that are totally wrong? Can you see how the business owner, the charter captain, might be losing business, might be losing that valuable repeat business because the experience was so bad?

More importantly, can you see how the Flawless Execution

Model can be put to work in the specialized world of marlin fishing? This is a fast-moving, chaotic, dangerous environment, often populated with strangers and novices. Plan-brief-execute-debrief. The pleasure of fishing, the feeling of accomplishment when you land a marlin—all the reasons why someone spends their precious time and hard-earned money on the charter are at stake, not to mention lives.

Well, it was like a bell going "ding!" above their heads. They saw the benefits immediately. They know half their business is one-time customers, but they never thought about what might be turning their customers off. These people fish for a living. They know where everything is and what everything does and, by gosh, they just assumed we did too. But it went beyond that. They assumed every crew member they signed on knew what to do, too, but in truth, they really don't. Fishing is plagued with transients. Captains do double back flips if they can keep a crew together for more than a couple of weeks. But every boat is configured a little differently, so the captain saw a need not only for the Flawless Execution cycle but also for a briefing guide for new crew members.

Flawless Execution makes things go smoothly and saves time when time is precious. By using it in marlin fishing we might one day see a crisp, smart, polished, charter operation that is the national leader in the industry.

I finished what I had to say, and it didn't take more than a second before I started to hear the ideas. "The briefing could take place before the anglers leave the dock in the morning," said one. Another said, "We would probably land more of the fish we hook." A third said, "We *do* have injuries, don't we?" and so on. This was no corporate boardroom. But Flawless Execution was already changing their lives.

That's marlin fishing. Now to medicine. No one needs to be told about lives in the field of medicine. Few people have any idea the extent to which executional mistakes make the job of saving lives a heck of a lot harder than it needs to be (and already is). In truth, studies show that deaths due to medical error could range between 98,000 and 250,000 patients a year.

Just as marlin fishing has its specialized problems, so too does medicine. One is called hand-offs. When you work in a fast-moving, chaotic environment, like the fighter pilot environment or, in this case, the hospital environment, your job requires that you hand off data. I'll over-simplify to make the point. When I got into my jet and taxied out to the active runway, I got a final weather brief. Winds, direction, density altitude. Rarely did I have a hand-off problem here. Let's count the hand-offs in just a simple weather report. The meteorologist gathers data from the reporting stations and posts the weather. That's one hand-off. Then weather officer takes that report and is briefed. Another hand-off. The weather officer then briefs the squadron in the briefing room. Another hand-off. Then, out on the runway, we get another update—another hand-off.

Weather hand-offs usually go okay, but hand-offs in the fighter community can get critical fast. Let me give you an example from an aircraft carrier. Fighters can't launch on the thrust of their engines alone. They need the catapult to give them an extra 20,000 or 30,000 pounds of thrust, and they need twenty knots of wind to get enough airspeed to climb. The amount of pressure in the catapult piston, however, is completely dependent on the wind velocity across the deck and the weight of the fighter. If you have a data hand-off problem calculating the catapult stroke, you can have a serious problem fast. Let's say the refuelers load 15,000 pounds of fuel into the jet when the instructions were for 10,000 pounds. If that happens, the catapult officer will dial-in pressure for a jet 5,000 pounds lighter than the jet sitting on the deck. When the cat fires, there isn't enough oomph to launch the fighter and a $25 million F/A-18 goes into the drink. That's called a *cold cat*. In this case, the cause was a faulty data hand-off.

The important thing is, if you aren't really religious about the way you hand off data, after it gets handed off three or four times, it degrades incredibly. Let's say that you start feeling bad. You call up your family physician and say, "I don't feel good." The family physician talks to you and says, "Oh, you need some antibiotics." In this day and age, that doctor is not even going to see you. You just call him up and you talk and he calls in a precautionary pre-scription and you go to the drug store and you take some antibi-otics. Another week goes by, and you're still feeling rotten. As a matter of fact, you have a terrible night, and your wife drives you to the ER. The ER doc says, "Hey, what's wrong?"

"Well, I've got these pains. I haven't been feeling good."

"Has the doctor been giving you any medicine?"

"Yeah, he prescribed some type of antibiotic but I'm not really sure what it was."

So he writes down in the report whatever it is that he thinks that you're talking about. "The patient's been on this drug; still has chest pains. I recommend two cc of this," and puts it in the chart. Then you get processed out of the ER into an outpatient bed.

You go to the outpatient bed. The nurse pulls the chart and says, "Well, the doctor said they thought you were on this and I can't read his writing, but I think he said twenty cc of this, in-stead of two cc of this, administered every other day."

And all of a sudden, you're feeling very bad. You have another doctor come in and look at you and, eventually, another diagno-sis is made and another medicine prescribed, and now this medi-cine can kill you. Error chains. Poor hand-offs.

The solution? The Flawless Execution engine. By mentally staying inside the plan-brief-execute-debrief cycle, the individual keeps their SA high, puts the chaotic environment into a process, and manages information with a higher degree of sensitivity. He or she will make fewer mistakes because of an organized, systematic process for managing the flow of unexpected events and his or her reaction to it.

Charles Denham, MD (who, not surprisingly, is also a pilot), helps hospitals and physician groups execute better. His mission is to make the medical community a community of Leaning-Forward fighter pilots who execute flawlessly, who sharply reduce the medical error chains. Says Denham, "Applying the principles of Flawless Execution has a real place in healthcare. Why? Because you have multiple players who are working in a high-stress, high-fatigue environment, dealing with complex packages of information. Really good surgeons make sure all the players understand what they're about to accomplish. And they're double checking, orchestrating the procedural work, maintaining a position of readiness and anticipation, very much like the environment on an aircraft carrier."

Continues Denham, "The five *rights* in medicine are the *right* patient, the *right* drug, the *right* route, the *right* dose, and the *right* time. The medical community knows all this, and they're dealing with these five rights, but in fact, there are harmful events that occur outside of these five rights. As an example, if a doctor doesn't have right information about you, you come in, and I prescribe the right drug to the right patient with the right dose at the right time, I can satisfy all the five rights, but I didn't know that your kidneys aren't working. The fact that I didn't know that, or somebody *did* know it but didn't communicate it to me—that's what we call a hand-off problem. Communication breakdowns and bad hand-offs are very common causes in adverse events in medicine."

However, by following the Flawless Execution cycle, the complex, rapidly changing, time-compressed environment of a hospital can become a ballet of precision moves. Before one staff comes on and another leaves, one group is debriefing and the other picking up the lessons learned and briefing their upcoming shift. Here's what we do when an ambulance arrives. Here is what we do when six patients hit the door all at once. Here's our checklist for triage, for medication, for moving data, for taking breaks. Here are our motherhoods and our standards. Here's the environment. We've got a rock concert tonight so expect some drug and alcohol–related events, and we've got rain so expect some car accidents and trauma injuries. By adding fifteen minutes to the management of shift changes and the inflow and outflow of practitioners on the floor, everyone saves time, things are more efficient, chaos is worked out of the system, contingencies are discussed with scripted responses, and the death rate due to errors drops. Denham knows this better than anyone—he's leading the charge. Through his work and training of other hospitals, he's helping cut the rate of medical errors leading to patient fatalities.

How, then, does Flawless Execution work for you?

As individuals, each of us is in the middle of perhaps a half-dozen Flawless Execution cycles. In my day-to-day activity I have at least five execution cycles going on at once. I have my workout cycle going, my corporate cycle going, our new product cycles going, my personal financial cycle going, and my travel plans going.

Interestingly, my personal cycles are not working at the same level, nor will they be for you. Each cycle is at a different level of maturity. Why? Because you bring to each cycle different experiences, different levels of accumulated learning experiences. I have almost ten years of accumulated learning experiences when it comes to running our core business. My Flawless Execution cycle on Afterburner, Inc. is mature and operates on a very high level. The words are familiar, the patterns are familiar, and the errors stand out like a sore thumb. My situational awareness is not just high—it's intense. I can take a problem anywhere in our company, quickly find a solution, and just as quickly weave that solution into our standards, while at the same time picturing in my head the thousands of ways throughout our company things will in small increments be affected. That's a very mature execution cycle.

But that's not always possible. As our company goes into a new business segment, we find ourselves on unfamiliar ground. Our knowledge base is limited; our accumulated learning experiences are almost nil. This execution cycle is moving slower, operating on a lower plane. I don't have the experiences to know with any certainty how one decision might affect another. I can't make decisions with the same confidence I can on my other cycle. I need to get up to speed, understand subtleties quickly. *But I can see my deficiencies because I have a process.* I see my weakness because I have a process that tells me I need more data. I need to mature my new product cycle so that as I act on it and think things through and prepare to go into this new business segment, I start moving my SA up a notch and my successful outcomes up an even bigger notch.

I said that I have a training cycle, and I do. I want to be in shape and maintain a certain weight, and I want to have a mix of cardiovascular exercise and muscle toning in my fitness routine. But I also travel and have too many dinner parties and these things work against my fitness cycle. Worse, in the beginning, when I knew almost nothing about training, I wasn't sure how anything interrelated. My cycle hadn't matured. Yes, I knew how to feed back lessons learned, and when I saw my weight hit a flat line, I knew how to dig down to the root causes and adjust my fitness plan. Beyond that, I was a neophyte.

But that's exactly how the cycle pays for itself. Instead of taking six months or a year to work through all the interrelated issues of a balanced fitness plan, I knew how to accelerate my learning experiences. By debriefing myself honestly—utterly honestly—I had a plan that was giving me the results I wanted within a few weeks of starting it up. Now that cycle is mature, I can make smart trade-offs, I stick to it, I have discipline, and I've never felt better in my life.

The point is that Flawless Execution works in us as individuals. You set out your life goals (Future Picture) and your personal centers of gravity in your system. Then you produce a Flawless Execution cycle around your daily responsibilities. Around and around this cycle spins, providing you with an internal clock, internal checks-and-balances, an internal method of accelerating your path toward your Future Picture.

I have several cycles going on at once. Fitness is important to me. In this case I have a clear, high-resolution fitness Future Picture. Less than 195 pounds, body fat less than 10 percent, thirty-four-inch waist, cholesterol less than 180, and visible abdominal muscles. Remember Renoir's picnic or that perfect ballpark hot dog? Using the strategies in this book, I looked at my external and internal systems that would stand in my way; I looked at my centers of gravity. My travel schedule and lack of good exercise facilities in hotels. Restaurant meals. Late night client dinners and cocktails. The excuse that there just aren't enough hours in the day to get it all done and by the end of the day I am just too tired to work out, so I'll hit it tomorrow.

Realizing that I had to attack these centers of gravity in parallel, I went to work. Here's my plan. I will attempt to schedule my seminars all in the same week and try to stay home every other week, so I can get a routine going. On the road I will book hotels close to large, well-known gyms. If there is not a gym close by, I will adjust my workout and focus on aerobic verses anaerobic. I will do conventional ground-based training to replace weights in this case, exercises like push-ups and leg squats without weights. I cannot get away from the restaurant thing but I will not eat anything heavy after 7 P.M. I will eat six smaller meals a day versus two and a half big meals, which will keep me from eating "big." At home I will work out with a trainer in order to get that extra rep that I did not have the discipline to get alone, and I will go to the gym regardless of my fatigue level if I have paid someone to work out with me.

With this strategy in mind, my fitness Flawless Execution cycle was ready to spin and attack these centers of gravity. If I need to trade-off, I can make smart trade-offs. If I eat a large meal or miss a workout or travel too much? I can insert the trade-offs into my cycle and make adjustments (just like fighter pilots make adjustments for bad weather on a mission or a fuel problem).

Another one of my cycles is knowledge. I wasn't a top-notch student in the classroom but I seem to have a natural affinity for education in my adult life so I joined the Young Entrepreneurs Organization and I make it a standard practice to sign-up for their lectures, travel programs and other learning experiences. With YEO I have been to Australia, Russia, France, and Canada and met more than a dozen people that I routinely interact with in my daily life.

Flawless Execution even works for the family, too. What do I mean by family? All of us have relationships and each one of our relationships has an impact on our Future Picture. If you were to map out your internal and external "family" system, you'd put on your list people like "parents," "children," "spouse" or "significant other," "friends," "downtime," "religion," and "civic duties." Every one of those are significant elements within your "family system." Each of those parts of your "family" impact your free time, your professional time, your workout time, your meals, your travel, your spiritual well being. You draw from those Elements and Centers of Gravity which help you move forward. And you give to those Centers of Gravity to help them move forward. In "family," Centers of Gravity overlap. A wife is in the husband's system; a husband is in the wife's. Both may have children and parents in their system. In family, Flawless Execution cycles need to be like a cluster of cogs turning a common shaft. Your Flawless Execution cycles need to *interrelate* with the cycles around it; they need to mesh.

Your workout cycle has to "work" with the schedules of others without degrading their cycles.

Your business cycle has to work with the business cycle of those in your system without degrading the others.

And all the better if the cycles actually improve one another. One of my close friends made a decision to become an Ironman athlete. He put in the hours, hit the pool, changed his diet and made the adjustments in his professional life that allowed him the personal time to train. Fast-forward six years. Six years later he's traveled all over the world competing, is absolutely fit, has incredible mental clarity (which has translated into six of his best years yet in business) and found his soulmate. Guess what she does? You bet—she runs the Ironman, too. They have woven together their personal cycles into an efficient, effective, smoothly functioning family cycle. These two now get more done together than they ever dreamed of as individuals.

Not a day goes by when I don't look at my cycle and see how it might be meshed with my family. This tends to show up when I plan some down time. I try to find ways to do things with my mother and father. I try to find ways to do things with my friends. The meshing comes by putting together something that's an integral part of my internal cycle with theirs. Good example: a fishing trip. I know it's tremendous fun for my friends but it's also a vital part of my own recreational cycle. Planning a weekend on my boat down in Florida meshes our two cycles.

When it comes to family, our Future Pictures have to be painted with our children and our spouses and our parents, etc. If we don't, we'll be personally frustrated when attempting to achieve our goals—and very likely an irritant to the ones we care about most.

IT'S IN ALL OF US

To stay ahead in the rapidly changing, fast-moving, intensely competitive world of business, you want your experiences to pay off faster than the experiences of your competition. You want to be sharper than the other guy, to be a better closer, to have a better *feel* for a customer, to make fewer mistakes—to operate on a higher plane than anyone else. As I said in the first chapter, it's the process that counts. The process is your tool. The process helps you get ahead, and that process is called Flawless Execution. You set it up in yourself. You give yourself time to run through it in your head. You make quiet time to debrief yourself. You stay honest with yourself. You feed your lessons learned back into the process, and you go out and do it again tomorrow.

The truth is, people want to do better. It's human nature. Millions of us are trying to lose weight. Millions of us bought a self-help book last month. Millions of us made New Year's resolutions. Millions of us received a promotion or a pay increase or started a company—and millions more will do it tomorrow. It's all about the basic drive to better ourselves.

But it doesn't have to be hard, and that's the message. So much of what makes us better is literally locked inside of *us*! Flawless Execution and all of the associated tools simply show you a path of least resistance to the person within that wants to get out and strut. Fighter pilots come from hundreds of different backgrounds and are born in countless cultures, but they all attain a level of execution most would think impossible. It's simply because they follow a process that unlocks the skills they need to excel. That's all there is to it. The skills are inside of us; the Flawless Execution process simply gives you a set of keys to work the locks.

That said, Flawless Execution is a demanding taskmaster. It's an overarching way to live. When you decide to make something a pattern for life, you have to start from scratch and let the process, the pattern, guide you. Build your schedule—and your life—around Flawless Execution. Then expect great things. Millions before you have. The essential ingredients are in all of us.

► INDEX